GARDEN
OF YOUR
DREAMS

CHARLIE ALBONE

GARDEN OF YOUR DREAMS

A practical guide to your best
outdoor transformation ever

murdoch books

Sydney | London

CONTENTS

WELCOME...

*G*arden of Your Dreams is a practical, user-friendly guide to the process of designing a garden that will enrich your life and change the way you live. It may sound cheesy, but a great garden will do just that.

An outdoor sanctuary should be a special and personal space to which you and your family and friends can retreat – a refuge from everyday life that only you and your loved ones can visit. Look out at your garden right now – is it a sanctuary? Or is it an overgrown mess, a plain bit of grass with no stand-out features or simply tired and boring? Well, imagine if it looked amazing and had everything you always wanted in an outdoor space. If this were your garden, wouldn't you want to be in it all the time?

I find that spending time outdoors in a gorgeous garden is the best form of physical and emotional self-care; the day fades away, and you get the chance to reset and repair. Although you may not consider yourself an expert gardener now, once you have designed and created your dream garden, you'll be pleased to know that it comes with a free set of green thumbs.

WHAT'S IN THE BOOK?

I'LL TAKE YOU THROUGH THE PROCESS AS WELL AS THE TIPS AND TRICKS I FOLLOW WHEN CREATING A BEAUTIFUL GARDEN THAT WILL PULL YOU OUTSIDE, INCREASE YOUR HOME'S LIVEABILITY AND IMPROVE YOUR WELLBEING. THE BOOK IS BROKEN INTO EIGHT SECTIONS, COVERING EVERYTHING YOU NEED TO KNOW FROM HOW TO PLAN YOUR GARDEN THROUGH TO CHOOSING THE BEST PLANTS FOR YOUR SPACE.

My story

This section describes how – thanks to a chance meeting – I became a gardener, and from there a landscape designer. I have been lucky enough to share my love of gardening on television, to compete at The Royal Horticultural Society (RHS) Chelsea Flower Show and to work in countries across the globe. Surprisingly, it all started with a car accident.

Where do I start?

Working out what you actually want from a space is one of the hardest things to do when designing your own garden. This chapter will walk you through that process and help you to create a priority list for your final dream garden. Once you know what you are trying to achieve, working out how it will actually look is equally important. I discuss the most common garden styles – from formal to tropical – and provide real-world examples so you can see the theory in practice.

It's all in the planning

Ideas and lists are great, but how on earth do you fit all of the elements into a landscape design? Carrying out a site analysis and creating a concept plan are musts before starting any new garden, regardless of whether it's big or small. Don't worry if you can't draw or use a fancy design program on a computer – I can't, either! You can still come up with a decent concept plan for your dream garden, and I'll show you how.

Entertaining spaces

Outdoor entertaining is a way of life in Australia. Especially when it's warm, you often find that you spend most of your time in your garden when you want to relax and connect with family and friends. This chapter will explore the various options available to you – from garden furniture and firepits to shade structures – and show you how to create a dream entertaining space. There is also a special section on installing garden lighting, which is a great way to extend the time in which you can enjoy your outdoor area.

Small spaces

Making the most of small spaces is important for those people who love gardens but live in apartments, terrace houses and small inner-city homes. I'll let you in on the strategies I use – including tricking the eye with clever plant choices and placements – and reveal how even the tiniest of balconies or courtyards can become a peaceful green oasis.

Soil preparation

Soil is the most important element in any garden; it's the life force for your plants. All good gardens start with a healthy soil, so this chapter will take you through the steps to achieving this, no matter what you are working with. You'll be able to identify what kind of soil you have, as well as learn how to improve it through the addition of organic matter and fertilisers. And you might not even need soil at all, thanks to the no-dig system!

Plants and lawn

Plants make a garden come to life. They transform the space from a bunch of hard and uninviting building materials to soft and flowing garden beds, sweeping lawns and incredible entertaining spaces. Many people find it daunting to choose plants and place them in the garden, but this chapter will make it easy. You'll learn how to:

> **select the right plants for the right spots**
> **compose a delightful planting scheme**
> **save money on your plants**
> **grow your own plants from seed and cuttings**
> **create and maintain the perfect lawn.**

My top fives

Finally, I'll describe some of my fail-safe plants, from trees and shrubs to grasses and ground covers. If you're after an aromatic plant, a textural plant or a blooming plant, I've got you covered. And for those who are looking to design their garden with colour in mind, I've listed my go-to choices in silver, purple and yellow – as well as the ways to use these hues for the greatest impact.

My story

I remember the moment I fell in love with gardening: it was the first time I saw a small flower with snakeskin-like petals.

I was 18 and juggling two jobs – as a painter and decorator during the day, and pulling pints at The Crown in the evening. Late one night, I witnessed a car accident – a black Vauxhall Calibra, driven by a drunk driver, crashed into a pillar at the entry to a Mr Phillip Binding's house in Winscombe, a small village in the south-west of England. I knocked on the door the following day and, although I didn't catch the number plate, I described the unusual car to Mr Binding. He appreciated my assistance, and asked if I knew of anyone who could help him in his garden on weekends.

I was trying to save money to travel to Australia, so I jumped at the chance to earn a little more. My first job was collecting a bucket of sheep poo and mixing it with natural yoghurt, leaving this wonderful concoction out in the sun and then painting it on the newly repaired front pillar to help age the stonework. What a start in landscaping!

One day, I failed miserably while trying to cut perfectly manicured stripes in Mr Binding's grass with the lawnmower. But rather than shouting at me for destroying his lawn, he took me over to a sloping area of the lawn that he called 'the rise'. Then he knelt down and showed me the most incredible flower I had ever seen. It was a snake's head fritillary (*Fritillaria meleagris*), popping up through the grass. The texture of the inky purple bloom looked just like a snake's skin. My awe at this amazing thing growing from the ground sparked something in me – it was the moment I knew that I wanted to become a gardener.

EARLY INFLUENCES

I was born in Hong Kong in the 1980s. At that time, the bustling city – and especially the harbour – was dirty and polluted. You might be surprised to know that my love for landscapes actually began in Hong Kong. I spent the

Phillip Binding's house in Winscombe, England, features a picturesque garden and sloping lawn.

first 12 years of my life in the small fishing village of Sai Kung, in a relatively rural area, and this is probably why I think of Hong Kong as a green space rather than an enormous city.

When Hong Kong was handed back to China, we moved back to the United Kingdom and the rolling hills of Somerset. As a day pupil at Sidcot School, I enjoyed riding around the English countryside on horseback. This certainly influenced my love of the outdoors and my appreciation for nature.

My mother, who is a keen gardener, tried on multiple occasions to get me interested in the gardening life. Once she offered to pay me five pence per piece to move rocks around her garden for a project she was doing. She also tried to get my siblings and me to help in the vegetable patch, mainly to show us the paddock-to-plate ethos ... this backfired when we were served oversized and incredibly tough vegetable-stuffed marrow. I'm happy to say that my move into gardening has propelled me into the favourite-child position in our family, and now one of my most cherished things to do is spend time out in my garden with my mum when she comes over to visit.

With a love of the outdoors, minimal gardening skills but a rapidly growing passion for horticulture, I packed my suitcase and made Australia home for my 'gap year'. I did all the things backpackers do – drank too much, laid around getting sunburnt and did rubbish jobs for a bit of extra cash. I was having a beer with a mate one night when he mentioned his brother needed some help doing garden maintenance the next day, and was I interested? Of course I said yes, expecting that I would be mowing lawns, deadheading roses or pruning shrubs. However, a rude shock awaited me – I spent the whole day with a leaf blower in my hand, moving leaves from one end of the Coca-Cola factory car park in Parramatta to the other. I'm not sure if there is another nation that has a bigger infatuation with leaf blowers than Australia!

Towards the end of my gap year, I realised that Australia was the place for me and working outdoors was something I loved doing. I knew that I didn't want to hold a leaf blower my whole life, but I was keen to find out how I could work in horticulture.

STUDYING IN AUSTRALIA

I spent a year in England, working out how to get back to Australia. During this time, I built a garden for my mother. It included a raised patio with recycled paving slabs, bricks and anything else I could find, plus a feature flower garden and a natural pond. The pond took ages, as I found it difficult to get an even water level. It was fun working alongside my mum, and throughout the project the bud of interest in gardening was swelling (pardon the pun!). Not long after, I ended up back in Australia on a student visa.

I studied full-time at Ryde TAFE and achieved a Diploma of Horticulture and Landscape Design. The course was excellent, but, in all honesty, there's nothing like hands-on learning out in the field. This is where I really learned about how plants grow, what they need and how just one element – such as too much sun, slightly waterlogged soil, prevailing wind or sandy soil – can make a huge difference to plant growth. You can't be a good landscape designer if you're not a gardener first.

While at TAFE, I was employed by a landscape construction firm that really worked me to the bone. I didn't enjoy it at all, so I left and ended up working for myself, doing a bit of everything: applying my newly acquired design skills, taking on minor construction jobs and maintaining a few properties. It was a great way to learn! I was able to see each project from conception through to end product, and watch it continue to grow. As a garden matures, you can go back and assess what worked, what didn't and why, and these are the most valuable lessons for a designer and garden maker.

Once I finished TAFE, I started to focus on my own business, Inspired Exteriors, full-time. I had plenty of work and was designing and building a wide range of gardens. I didn't have a personal style at the time, but I loved creating different themes and styles of garden to suit each individual client. The early years really were about observing and learning, and I found that I enjoyed this and could quickly apply the lessons I had learned.

NEW OPPORTUNITIES

I was a member of the Australian Institute of Landscape Designers and Managers, and out of the blue I received an email that went out to all of its members asking if we wanted to audition for a role as a presenter for a television show. So I got my housemate to film me at one of my projects, and sent in the video. To cut a long story short, the show was *Selling Houses Australia* – and I got the job! With no previous television experience, I was actually terrible at the start. However, we did go on to film the show for 13 years, so I must have got better at it.

Working on television is an amazing experience, and it has given me so much: the ability to inspire others to try gardening, as well as a way to travel the country and meet all types of people. But hands-down the best thing television has done for me is to introduce me to my wife.

After two seasons of *Selling Houses Australia*, I was asked to host a new show called *The Party Garden*. While the premise of the show was great – renovate a garden and then have a big party in the new space – the reality was a bit of a disaster. However, interior designer Juliet Love was chosen as my co-host. I had seen pictures of Juliet and I thought she was perfection. Her first impression of me wasn't great, though – when I tried to make a joke about my car and the relative size of my manhood, it fell flat – but we are married now with two children, so something must have worked in my favour!

Our show had one season, but *Selling Houses Australia* continued on. By this time I had become a qualified tradesman and supervisor, and through my business I was designing and building lots of gardens. I was happy, as I could work in two different fields. Television is a quick in-and-out gig, working towards high-impact, often budget-conscious elements of a garden; on the flip side, creating a garden from nothing for my private clients allows me to spend time getting to know them, find out what they want from a garden and implement it in a manner that completely changes the way they live. Both are rewarding in different ways.

COMPETING AT CHELSEA

The annual RHS Chelsea Flower Show in London has long been a pinnacle of garden design and innovation, and it's every gardener's dream to exhibit there. In 2013, my brother's wedding happened to coincide with the event, so I hatched a plan to film a magazine-style show for the Lifestyle Channel, which gave me access to all the gardens (usually off-limits to everyone apart from judges and esteemed guests!). Walking through these amazing gardens that had been created in just three weeks and seeing how even the smallest detail can have an impact on the whole atmosphere of a space had a profound effect on me. From that moment on, I designed gardens in a completely different way.

I was back the following year to film a documentary about Australian garden designer Phillip Johnson and his team going for gold at the show. The garden was epic: a huge billabong with cascading waterfalls, a grotto and a floating studio, and it deservedly won 'best in show'.

During this visit, I met larger-than-life landscaper Mick Conway, who was helping out on the Australian build. We became friends and went on to build three gardens together at Chelsea. The first was for a hero of mine, Alan Titchmarsh, who was a pioneer of gardening on television in the United Kingdom. Helping on his build felt like a real honour. I worked closely with designer Kate Gould, and it was great to be digging, planting and pruning each plant to perfection. The thing about Chelsea is that you are surrounded by people who are the best at what they do, and they are more than happy to share their knowledge. I love that about horticulture – there is a real sense of camaraderie.

The following year, 2015, was my first attempt at a garden of my own at Chelsea. It was thrilling to be responsible for such a large show garden on the main avenue of the showgrounds. In all honesty, I thought I would only ever get one shot at making a garden in this magical place, so I decided to create one that really meant something to me. I designed a garden called 'The time in-between' which was dedicated to my father, who passed away when I was 17. This was my chance to tell him about what happened in my life after he died – it was a space to reconnect.

The garden was split into three sections. The first was a path wide enough to fit the whole family side-by-side, meandering through flowering plants I grow in my own garden at home. In the central part, a water feature slowly filled, stalled and then rapidly emptied, which replicated the emotions felt when someone close to you passes away. The final section at the rear of the garden was a sunken courtyard surrounded by solid sandstone pillars, each one representing an important person in my life. In the centre of the courtyard was a firepit that represented my wife and the fire within me, and the planting here became more foliage-based to direct the energy inwards and allow us to sit and really connect.

It was a hugely personal journey for me, from coming up with the garden concept and pitching it to companies for sponsorship, to organising the team to install it. The process was incredibly intense and stressful. Luckily, we made a TV show about it so I can now enjoy the memory of the garden, and my children will be able to watch the show when they get older.

We were awarded the second-highest medal: Silver Gilt. It was an amazing achievement! The thing I love about Chelsea is the feedback from the judges who hand out the medals. You are judged very strictly against the brief you have submitted with your application; not only do you have to meet that brief, but you also have to be horticulturally correct. For example, if you plant something in the shadow of a tree but it requires more sun, you get marked down. I was marked down for the ground cover between my stepping stones, as the judges said it needed to be a bigger clump so it wouldn't dry out. It really is a mix of science and art.

An army of helpers, including my wife and mum clipping the lawn with scissors, put the finishing touches on my second RHS Chelsea Flower Show garden in 2016.

A SECOND CHANCE

When I was invited back to submit a design for the show the following year, my wife couldn't believe that I was even going to consider it after what the last one had taken out of me. But I wasn't going to let the experience slip away, so back to the drawing board I went. I wanted to do something completely different. My first garden was a loose, flowing, emotive space, so this time it would be formal and tight.

I decided to design a space for a busy couple to retreat to after work, with a sunken lawn surrounded by layers of hedging and large box-head trees, plus a small courtyard with a feature garden bed connected to a pavilion with a floating roof. To tie the various areas together, a copper water rill ran around the courtyard, down the steps and around the lower sunken lawn. The project had its ups and downs, and I was let down by the company that supplied the copper for the water rill. Every garden at the show is built with precision, so when the copper arrived

and the measurements were off, the joints were wonky and ugly black silicone had been used to fill the gaps, I was in despair. We spent days trying to fix the issues, and ultimately we ran out of time to go over the garden in detail and tweak the tiniest elements. Despite this, we were awarded another Silver Gilt medal – and I can say that I am the only Australian-based landscape designer to exhibit at Chelsea two years in a row.

OPENING NEW DOORS

Soon after this, I was asked to design and implement a project in Hong Kong, which led to me being introduced to the owners of the Shangri-La Hotel group. They were impressed with my efforts and asked me to help with the redesign of the lobby of their flagship hotel in Singapore.

The famous Shangri-La Singapore has a huge 6-metre by 9-metre (20-foot by 30-foot) wall above the

The verdant wall at the Shangri-La Singapore has become a refreshing centrepiece of the lobby.

lobby bar, and the Japanese interior designer envisioned a new rock wall alive with planting. That's where I came in. The design process was fun, and I oversaw the build. Our stonemason, Callum Gray, and my team created a stunning piece of which we are very proud.

The Chelsea connection has sent me all over the globe, and I was even invited to design a garden at the world's largest garden expo in Beijing. With just 24 hours' notice, I drafted and submitted a design, and then watched from Australia as an excellent team of builders pulled it together.

The schedule I had to keep to ensure that all of these garden projects were delivered on time and to a high standard, as well as flying all over the country to film *Selling Houses Australia*, was taking its toll. I missed my family and they missed me, and my boys were starting to ask why I had to leave so often. So when I got a call from

Russell Palmer, the executive producer of TV show *Better Homes and Gardens*, I was interested. The pitch to become the new landscaper on the hit show got me excited – I would be telling stories and inspiring people to get into gardening, just like Phillip Binding and Alan Titchmarsh had done for me. It also meant that I could be at home a lot more. Although I knew that I would miss the team at *Selling Houses Australia*, going out on a high and moving towards a better quality of life for my family won hands-down.

So here I am now, writing this book in the hope that it will inspire you to give gardening a go. Before you read on, go outside and take in your garden. Close your eyes and think about what your dream garden would look like, how it would make you feel and how it might change your life. Hopefully, you'll pick up a few tips and tricks in this book to make that dream a reality.

PART ONE
PLANNING YOUR DREAM GARDEN

CHAPTER ONE

WHERE DO I START?

These days, everything happens so quickly in this fast-paced world. Having a smartphone ensures that knowledge (true or false) is always at our fingertips, and this makes us impatient. I mean, we get cranky if we have to wait too long for a coffee! We are ultimately after things that give us a quick fix, but these things can be unrewarding. Designing, building and looking after a garden, on the other hand, requires patience. Each part takes time. And anything that takes time is generally worthwhile.

I liken creating a garden to having a family, a marriage or a career. You need to nurture it for it to be a success. This process and investment means that it will obviously take more time than the quick fix; however, it will be exponentially more rewarding in so many ways.

I've been known to spend many an hour staring at survey plans and random pieces of paper, wondering where to start on a design. It's funny, people think I turn up to a job and know exactly what to do immediately because that's what they see me do on television, but in fact good design can take time. Don't get me wrong, there are moments when a flash of inspiration will come to me or, through my previous experiences, I'll know straight away what will or won't work, but there are also times when it's more of a challenge. More often than not, this is when I don't feel like I'm on the same page as the client I'm working for. When designing my own garden, the opposite happens: there is too much possibility, and it's hard to narrow it down to one cohesive idea.

Designing your own garden has the excellent benefit of you not having to articulate all of your ideas and concepts to somebody else. However, it also has the drawback of being too 'close to home', meaning that you're not able to be critical of the design, which can lead to a garden that has too much in it and doesn't feel curated or polished. Here, I'll show you how to get the balance just right.

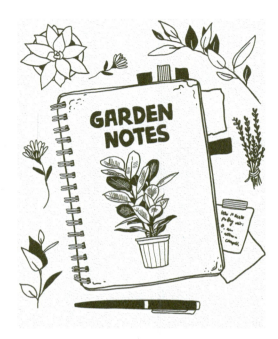

CREATE A WISH LIST

THIS IS THE CRITICAL FIRST STEP TO ACHIEVING A GARDEN WITH ALL THE ELEMENTS YOU WANT. IT INVOLVES ASKING YOURSELF TWO IMPORTANT QUESTIONS.

The first: *how do I want it to make me feel?* Most people think of their garden primarily as a practical space – somewhere to kick a ball, to eat or to swim. If you start to think about how you want to *feel* in the space, you'll approach the design with a different mindset.

I completely understand if you think this sounds like a bunch of designer hogwash: it does seem a bit woo-woo. But if you can build a garden that creates an emotional connection as well as providing a practical space ... well, this is the best garden of all. This connection will be important throughout the construction phase and beyond, as it will bond you to the space, and your emotional investment means that you will care for it more – and it will show.

Translating your feelings into a garden design could look something like this.

> **Happy:** a place to entertain family and friends, maybe with separate adults' and kids' zones
> **Safe:** soft planting and neutral tones
> **Private:** screening out the neighbours' properties, or creating a few small and intimate nooks
> **Chilled out:** zones to relax in, perhaps with a water feature
> **Excited:** entertaining spaces such as an outdoor dining area or a firepit; designer statements such as sculptural elements or dramatic lighting
> **Energised:** an open and free-flowing space, with room to run or work out
> **Alive:** elements with high visual impact, such as a stone wall or water feature.

Once you've worked out how you want your garden to make you feel, you're starting to think like a gardener – and you're halfway to nailing your wish list.

Adding personality to a garden is vital for creating emotion within the space, and you can do this by including items that mean something to you. Don't worry if they're not considered stylish, or even if others say they're ugly – if they mean something to you, then surround yourself with these things in your garden.

This stylish inner-city garden has a sense of character that is safe, private and fun.

'I want an explosion of interesting foliage that takes my breath away when I walk out the back door, fills me with pride when friends arrive and makes a great backdrop to outdoor living.'

'I want
a pool, a
pergola and
somewhere
to enjoy
a drink.'

The second important question is: *what do I really want to get out of my garden?* Answering this will make you focus on your priorities and how you want to use your garden. It may be the first time you've had the opportunity to create your own unique space, and the possibilities are endless.

Now to your wish list: the ultimate list of everything you want or desire in a garden. Think big, be bold, and don't leave anything out!

Your wish list might look like this:
> A swimming pool with a diving board
> A wisteria-covered outdoor dining area with a pretty ceiling of flowers that lets in the winter sun
> A perfect flat lawn for ball games and dogs
> A dream deck with room for cooking, eating and chilling
> A private zone to read and relax in, with plenty of screening from the neighbours.

Soak it all up

Don't be limited by your own imagination – there are plenty of different ways to find inspiration for your dream garden. Just for starters, the internet has a wealth of ideas: Google, Pinterest and Instagram, plus landscape and garden-design websites, are a rich mine of information. Start a virtual mood board, and collect all of your favourite images in one place so they're easy to find later.

Getting out and seeing real gardens is one of the best ways to find inspiration for your own garden. You can view plants in situ and understand their growth habits. If your plant knowledge is limited, take a walk around your neighbourhood. Gardens in your local area will have similar microclimates to yours, and you'll be able to see which species are likely to thrive in your garden.

There are many open gardens across the country, and those people who open their doors to the public often love to share their passion and knowledge with as many people as possible. So get out there and talk to the garden owners for some of the best advice you will ever receive.

I also really like to visit garden shows to see how other landscape designers are pushing the boundaries of design. You might not get heaps of practical ideas for your own garden, but you will be amazed at what is possible – and this may fuel your creativity.

Refining the dream

Of course, not everything on your wish list will be doable, but it's great to have aspirations. Editing a wish list is the hard part, but rather than cull items completely, I like to order the wish list by levels of importance: the must-haves at the top, and the nice-to-haves at the bottom. Common sense and a good dose of reality should also play a role in this step. You need to consider the amount of space you have and be realistic as to what will fit into your garden. For example, if you have a small space you're unlikely to be able to fit in a pool,

veggie patch, large formal lawn and a trampoline – something has to give. In the next chapter, we'll look at how to draft a plan that will help you reorganise your wish list further, as you take the actual size of each element and see if it will fit into your space with room to move around it.

Knowing your budget will help you refine your wish list further. There are many factors that go into determining your budget, and this is something I spend a lot of time talking to my clients about.

'I want a private sanctuary that envelops me with cool greens as I venture into its depths, where I can spend weekends and evenings relaxing and meditating.'

So, how much should I spend?

The only real answer to this is 'as much as you are comfortable spending'. I'm assuming that you see the value in gardens, as you're reading this book. For some people, a fabulous garden can potentially transform their home and way of living completely, and they're willing to spend any amount of money on it.

It's a good idea to get ballpark figures for different elements, so you can work out what can be achieved in your space. Remember to consider things such as access to the site, availability of materials and the level of finish you want, as they will all play a part in the final cost.

If you have a set budget and want to stick to it, I think it's a better option to do fewer elements executed to a higher standard than to go for more elements done on the cheap. Landscaping is just like building, with the added challenge that everything has to withstand the climate, so the level of quality in the build has to really stand the test of time.

If you're looking at reducing your costs, you could consider taking on some of the simpler grunt work yourself, as labour is the biggest expense when installing a garden. This might include digging, moving soil from one place to another, spreading mulch and cleaning up after tradespeople. The more you can do yourself, the further your money will go.

A garden transformation can add real value to your property, but you don't want to risk overcapitalising.

WHAT TO SPEND

IN GENERAL, THE HIGHER THE VALUE OF YOUR HOUSE WHEN COMPARED TO OTHER PROPERTIES IN YOUR AREA, THE MORE YOU CAN SPEND AND GUARANTEE A RETURN ON INVESTMENT. I TRY TO WORK TO THE FOLLOWING PERCENTAGES.

> **For houses at the lowest end of the market,** spend 2–3 per cent of the property value.
> **For houses in the low to middle part of the market,** spend 4–6 per cent of the property value.
> **For houses in the middle to high part of the market**, spend 7–9 per cent of the property value.
> **For houses at the highest end of the market,** spend up to 10 per cent of the property value.

Think about ongoing maintenance

Another element to consider when refining your wish list is the amount of time you can devote to maintaining your garden once it is up and running. Again, be realistic here! Almost every garden you see online will have had a professional gardener or gardeners tend to it, so be honest with yourself about how much you can feasibly do.

There are high-maintenance items such as vegetable patches, flowering perennial gardens and water features that all require constant care. I'm all for giving these things a go if you're a novice gardener, but be warned that there will be hits and misses. You'll discover more about gardening and plant growth with the misses than the hits, so if you're willing to learn then go for it.

If you want to limit any failures, opt for low-maintenance plants. You could also allocate some of your budget to the establishment and ongoing maintenance of planting by an external company.

WHAT STYLE OF GARDEN DO I WANT?

Once you have your wish list nailed down, you need to consider what style of garden you're after. One way of doing this is to group all of your inspo images together to see if a theme emerges. Look at the elements you like about the designs you have picked, and group similar elements together. Often the style of a garden is identified through the choice of materials, plants, colours and finishes, such as lighting and fabrics, rather than just the particular layout of the space.

When thinking about style, remember that every garden is unique, and you don't need to replicate a style leaf for leaf. This is one of the things I love about landscape design: every job I turn up to will be different from the job I just left. The style of gardens might be similar, but each garden will have it's own individual elements that make it unique. Use a style as inspiration; copy the parts you really like, but make them work for your specific space.

Taking into account the architectural style of your house may help you choose a garden style. For example, a Federation house might be enhanced by a formal garden, while a weatherboard house could be refreshed and modernised by a Hamptons-style garden. When you have complementary styles, they tend to sit more comfortably together than those that juxtapose. It is possible to blend different styles of architecture and garden, but it can be a difficult and costly task to do well.

As there are so many styles to choose from – everything from tropical to cottage to coastal – for the majority of gardens it's best to pick one style and stick to it. This ensures that there is a seamless feel throughout the whole space, and the garden looks brilliant rather than budget. However, if you have a large garden, creating different 'rooms' is a good way to mix it up and apply different styles.

I loved designing this space. While working with the various levels of the garden, I got to use a mix of materials such as stone, timber and concrete.

One garden style that seems to be able to create a range of emotions and offer practicality at the same time is the contemporary Australian garden. Australia is not naturally tied by cultural heritage to any one specific style of garden design, so a style has evolved that takes the best parts of conventional garden styles

CAN'T AFFORD A GRAND NEW STYLE?

Here are three simple things you can do if you don't have the money for a whole-garden transformation.

> Give the garden a good clean-out, as a tidy space is more inviting.

> Create an area for gathering – it doesn't have to be over-the-top.

> Start small with your plants, and propagate from them as they grow.

and combines them all to achieve a look that is fresh, inviting, sympathetic to its surroundings, modern and cutting edge. Interestingly, the Australian style is not climate-based – it's first and foremost about the overall look, then the choice of plants is adapted accordingly to suit the climate.

Formal gardens

Formal gardens have structure and clean lines reminiscent of those you might see at baroque-style palaces such as Versailles. Originally created as a symmetrical form to be admired from a palatial balcony, this style has evolved over the years to become a softer, more engaging space, and one that suits many different styles of architecture. The bones, however, have stayed the same: strong lines, geometric shapes and symmetry, often based around a central feature such as a fountain or sculpture.

My opinion of formal gardens has changed drastically over the years. When I first started out learning about garden design, I found them boring and repetitive; I was more about features that shocked and grabbed the eye. Heavily influenced by the experimental style of Diarmuid Gavin – who included in his designs things such as a stainless steel spaceship in the middle of a lawn, and aubergine rendered walls – I was more interested in trying to do things that hadn't been done before: elliptical bench seating, feature walls made from copper and glass panels, different combinations of plants. Nothing was off limits.

Later in my career, I discovered a real appreciation for formal gardens and the serenity they bring to a space – they have a calming influence and encourage an emotional connection. I love their structure as it gives a sense of knowing to a space, which in turn makes it feel safe. My wife says my new-found love of formal gardens was due to her influence, too, and she's probably not wrong there.

Old-style formal gardens – like those you'd see around European castles – are a bit too much for me on a day-to-day basis, but I love the combination of structured hedging and soft, floaty planting. It's totally fine to take a style and add your own flavour or flair to it.

My RHS Chelsea Flower Show garden in 2016 was a very formal affair. I softened the clipped hedges with perennial flowering plants.

A grand old dame

This massive 1940s house has multiple extensions, and is made even more imposing by the fact that it is raised up on the block. To match, I went big with landscaping a formal garden. Huge sandstone columns flank the entryway to set the tone. The pathway and paving stones throughout the project are 2-metre by 1-metre (6-foot by 3-foot) solid slabs of sandstone that required an industrial vacuum lifter to move them into place. There is a 9-metre (29½-foot) high fireplace in the central courtyard, and we even renovated an old Sydney monorail carriage into a bespoke getaway in the garden! All of the elements sound grandiose on paper; however, they sit comfortably in the space alongside the architecture of the home.

3 MUST-HAVES FOR A FORMAL GARDEN

> Straight lines
> Central features
> Symmetry

PLANNING YOUR DREAM GARDEN

Hamptons-style gardens

Similar in many ways to a formal garden style, but with a coastal twist, this style is very popular at the moment. It really complements beach-style architectural elements such as weatherboards, ornate metals and a soft colour palette, often in shades of grey. Hints of formality come with low box (*Buxus*) hedging to garden beds but also from an abundance of flowers such as hydrangeas and gardenias.

The thing that sets a Hamptons-style garden apart from others is the strong sense of structure in the layout, with a focus on clutter-free symmetry. Lawns are heavily used – normally as the central feature of the design – as they give a sense of space and airiness to the garden.

I like to use this style for the front of a property. Front gardens have the ability to simply look nice – they don't need any practical elements to them, as you often just walk through them or look at them from the street. They set the tone for the property, so they need to be a feature that creates impact.

3 MUST-HAVES FOR A HAMPTONS-STYLE GARDEN

> Stone, timber and metal combinations
> Formal hedges with soft-flowering plants as support
> Relaxed lawn areas for spilling out onto during warm summer nights

3 MUST-HAVES FOR A COASTAL GARDEN

> Well-aged materials, such as silvered timber
> Hardy plants that are native to coastal areas
> Free-form layout that follows the natural lie of the land

Coastal gardens often have to work with a natural slope.

Coastal gardens

Coastal gardens tend to be relaxed and informal, often with sweeping decks. There is a focus on natural materials that have been left to age gracefully, such as silvered and weathered timber. These elements are offset by hardy, wind-tolerant plantings – such as flax (*Phormium* species), westringias and ornamental grasses – placed in free-flowing garden beds.

The topography of coastal gardens is often sloping. Because of this, the layout of the garden needs to work with the lie of the land and not fight against it. Water retention in the soil may be an issue.

Cacti and succulents come in a variety of shapes and sizes, and they add visual interest to drought-tolerant gardens.

Drought-tolerant gardens

The major benefit of a drought-tolerant garden is that it's more likely to survive during periods when water is scarce – a common occurrence in Australia. It uses low-maintenance plants that are able to retain water reserves, such as cacti and succulents.

Often mistaken for a style of planting, the drought-tolerant garden maximises water use through sweeping open spaces where textures in the surfaces provide interest. Water-penetrable surfaces such as gravel are often used, and architectural plants are cleverly placed to draw the eye through the garden. There is often a water feature to capture what is not naturally available – almost as a tease.

3 MUST-HAVES FOR A DROUGHT-TOLERANT GARDEN

> Natural stone or boulders
> Plants that retain water in their leaves or trunks
> A water feature, such as a bird bath

Tropical gardens

If you live in a temperate region, having a tropical garden conjures up the feeling of being on holiday and getting away from it all. A combination of large-leafed plants – such as philodendrons, elephant's ears (*Alocasia* species) and bananas (*Musa* species) – and rustic materials (such as recycled timber, aged metal and roughly dressed stone) will give you a tropical garden of delight.

Tropical gardens are really all about creating a sense of tranquillity, and this can be done in many different ways. The introduction of water helps to calm the senses, while meandering pathways through the plants add a feeling of serenity. You can also create a retreat or nook as your own private oasis.

3 MUST-HAVES FOR A TROPICAL GARDEN

› A relaxed hotel vibe
› Lots of plants with
  big leaves
› Rustic finishes, such
  as rough-hewn stone

Cottage gardens

One of my favourite garden styles is the cottage garden. The layout is informal and relaxed, with traditional materials such as stone used in rustic ways (for example, as cobblestones). The focus is on the array of ornamental and edible planting – incorporating a wide variety of perennials, in many different colour and texture combinations – which is normally very dense in its layout.

It takes time to learn the composition of cottage gardens and how the plants are grown together to maximise the impact of the overall picture – as well as how to create detailed vignettes – but these skills must be perfected for a good cottage garden. Pathways are often tight to bring you closer to the plants, while greenery and flowers also surround any sculptures and water features.

Overflowing with charm

Red Cow Farm, located in the NSW Southern Highlands, is one of my favourite gardens, not only in Australia but also the world. Created by Ali Mentesh, it is the epitome of a cottage garden. Before Ali and his partner, Wayne, got their hands on the property, it was a flat cow paddock. Now an abundance of flowers intermingle and spill out from enormous garden beds, creating a tapestry of plants that is layered, textural and simply irresistible. Crazy paving leads you through the garden, but cleverly the pathways are narrow to slow you down and get you closer to the planting design. In some areas, lawn is used to give breathing space to the planting design while maintaining a soft approach to the overall finish of the garden.

3 MUST-HAVES FOR A COTTAGE GARDEN

> An abundance of densely packed plants
> An informal layout
> Accessibility to plant life along narrow paths

I love this glimpse down my driveway. Evergreen alders (*Alnus* species) flank the curve, while a sculptural pear sits comfortably beneath the trees.

So, what style of garden do I have?

My garden at Flowerfield Farm is one of my favourite places in the whole world. Just before my wife and I had our first child, we purchased a 2-hectare (5-acre) property just outside of Sydney. We bought it for the garden (or I did, anyway). The property has large hedges, mature deciduous trees, a sweeping driveway and large lawns. The best part is the layout – the utility areas are in the right place, the trees are in perfect locations, and the house is orientated to make the most of the surrounding greenery. I, of course, have added to the garden.

The garden has a typically country style, the tone set by the mature trees and hedging. Country gardens are soft and free-flowing, and they have a sense of imperfection that makes them perfect to me. I love flowers in all shapes and sizes, and have tried to grow as many as possible in my little slice of heaven (hence the name, which my wife came up with). Designing with flowers is one of the hardest ways to design a garden bed, as you really need to know your plants. Working out when a plant will flower and how it will look in comparison to the surrounding plants and their flowering times really tests your horticultural knowledge. This skill is one that takes constant learning, through watching and adapting.

I love the special feeling I get when I arrive at Flowerfield Farm – instant relaxation and a sense of coming home. I created an area with a strong emotional connection to my family to reinforce this. The pergola was a collapsed structure when we purchased the house, so I renovated it in the country-garden style. I added elements such as the water feature to bring in wildlife (it's magical when birds arrive for a bath while you're dining alfresco). And the firepit (which represents my wife) comes from the garden I created at the RHS Chelsea Flower Show in 2015.

PLANNING YOUR DREAM GARDEN

5 QUESTIONS TO ASK YOURSELF BEFORE DESIGNING YOUR GARDEN

> How do I want my garden to make me feel?

> What do I want to get out of my garden?

> How much time do I have for ongoing maintenance?

> How much do I want to spend?

> What style of garden do I prefer?

This pergola had decayed and collapsed before we bought the property, so I renovated it and now we use it every day.

CHAPTER TWO

IT'S ALL IN THE PLANNING

When you're starting an exciting project like a garden renovation, it's tempting to jump right in, pick up a shovel and just get digging! But my experience has taught me that good results come from good design, and for that a process needs to be followed. Trust me: I have tried both approaches, and the one that takes a little more time gives exponentially better results.

Corralling all of your ideas into one space can be tricky. It's great that you have a wish list, but how do you get it all into *your* garden? What you need next is a base plan: a kind of mud map drawn to scale to make sure everything fits properly, that you can eventually develop further into a landscape concept plan. This concept plan will allow you to assess all of your individual ideas to make sure they'll work in practice, and to eliminate items that may not work or are not as important to you as other elements.

Having a plan will also give you a reference point to go back to, so you don't veer off track during the construction stage. I often see this happen when projects aren't planned properly: different ideas get introduced along the way, and you end up with a Frankenstein's garden of mismatched styles, ideas and finishes.

The good news is that drafting a base plan is easy, and you need very little skill to do it – just a good imagination.

PULLING TOGETHER YOUR BASE PLAN

BEFORE YOU GET STARTED, YOU'LL NEED A FEW BASIC TOOLS ON HAND: A SCALE RULER, TWO TAPE MEASURES (PREFERABLY ONE LONG AND ONE SHORT), PLUS PLENTY OF PAPER AND PENCILS.

It's crucial that your plan is drawn to scale. Using a proper scale ruler allows you to take a measurement outside, and then translate that onto paper inside. If everything is measured and then translated at the same scale, then you'll have a drawing that correlates exactly to what you want to happen outside. For example, you might choose to work at a metric 1:100 scale, which means 1 metre in your garden will correlate to 1 centimetre on paper.

You can work to whatever scale fits the paper you are drawing on, but I would recommend making your drawing as big as possible – perhaps A3 size – so it's easier to see and use. It also means that you don't have to be as detailed with your drawing – which is perfect for a non-drawer like me!

To start, you'll need an outline of your garden perimeter. If your project or garden is small, you can have a go at drawing this up yourself, otherwise you can engage a professional surveyor who will give you an accurate result. In 20 years of drawing plans, I think I've only ever drafted one garden that was perfectly square, so simply measuring the fence line won't do. You need to take your long measuring tape (or a piece of string) and run it down the middle of the garden from one end to the other. Then start at one end and measure out to the boundary on both sides of the tape. Try to work at a right angle to the centre line, as this will make your measurements more accurate. Do this at intervals of 50 centimetres (20 inches) along the tape, all the way to the end. Then when you come to putting this on paper, draw a straight line down the middle of the page that correlates to the length of the garden, and mark up every 50 centimetres (20 inches) in scale, drawing out all of the measurements you have taken.

You'll also need to plot any fixed items that can't or won't be removed from the current garden. This includes buildings, trees, walls, easements, gas and water outlets, sewers, powerlines and underground pipes. Measure these off the same central line, and then transfer them to your base plan.

Once every item is plotted on your base plan, make as many copies as you can. You'll be scribbling ideas on the paper and reworking them over and over again, so you may need a few spare plans.

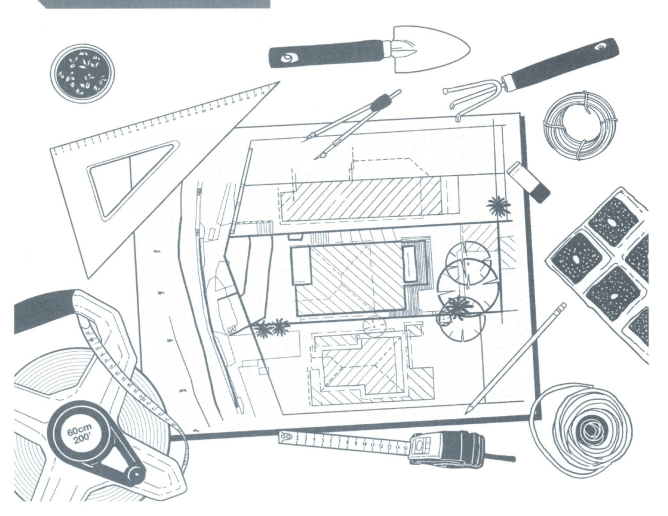

SITE ANALYSIS

This is your chance to really get in tune with the space you are about to design, and it's best done slowly, with time for reflection. Spend time out in the garden, and look for elements that might have an impact on the design. I like to call this 'coffee time' or – as the day goes on – 'gin and tonic time'. Take one of your base-plan copies so you can scribble on it with a pencil, and consider the following elements.

Sun and shade

Tracking the sun across the garden throughout the day will tell you where the hot spots are, and at what time of day. This will have an impact on where you locate your entertaining zone, children's play area, vegetable patch or swimming pool, and also what your plant choices will be. Tracking the sun means that you are also identifying the shady spots, which again will influence your choices for certain elements in the garden design. (Note that the sun's elevation changes throughout the year – see the Seasons section on page 58 for more information.)

Watching the sun move around the garden is a commitment, and may require several coffees or G&Ts, but I guarantee that it's time well spent. Try to focus on the severity of the sun, and how it makes you feel. Do you want to filter the sun? Would you prefer more sunlight in the garden? Is the light better in the morning or the afternoon?

Soil

Understanding the soil condition in various spots throughout the garden is a vital part of getting a garden design right. Dig a hole, and take a handful of soil: is it clay, silt or sand, or a combination (called loam)? You should also look out for water content: is the soil sample sodden and smelly, or dry and powdery? How much wildlife is living in your soil? The presence of worms and other soil dwellers indicates excellent soil health. The type of soil you have will affect many of the choices you make in your new garden. See Chapter 5 for more on soil identification.

Heights and landform

Very few blocks of land are dead flat; usually there will be a slope or fall in the ground somewhere. This may be at a gradient you are comfortable with, or your dream of a bowling-green lawn may require levelling and retaining work. Some blocks may require extensive retaining walls to create usable spaces – the upside is that these features can add visual interest and a dynamic feel that a flat block might not be able to provide. Sloping ground also tells you how water moves around your site: higher points will naturally be drier than lower points, which can hold moisture, and this may influence construction methods and plant choices. Make a note of any boggy areas, as these are generally harder to fix than dry areas.

Neighbours and noise

Most of us want a private garden, so it can be an oasis where we escape from the outside world. If you can, it's a good idea to plan to remove or screen out any unsightly elements that affect the feel of your garden. When I draw up a base plan, I use different coloured pencils to represent the severity of the impact that the surrounding properties have on the site. For example, I might draw a neighbours' shed casting shade over the boundary in orange, and an upstairs window overlooking the back lawn in red. It's also a great idea to consider future developments and the effects they might have on your dream garden. If that large empty block next door could potentially get rezoned for low-rise apartments, you might want to consider changing the focus of your aspect or looking at your screening options.

Traffic noise may also affect the way you use your outdoor space. I often get asked what plants minimise noise the best, but sadly plants on their own aren't hugely effective. To have any meaningful effect on noise from a busy road, you would need almost a kilometre (½ a mile) of dense forest to lower the decibels to a point where the noise wasn't an issue. Planting does, however, provide a visual barrier that has an effect on how you perceive noise, so I like to strategically plant tall trees and shrubs if noise is an issue. The sound of flowing water will also help to mask any offensive noise, so think about installing a water feature, too.

Prevailing winds

A windy garden can be a very uncomfortable place to spend time in. Windbreaks – in the form of plants, built screens or a combination of the two – may need to be included to reduce the effects of wind in key areas. Wind not only affects how you entertain, but can also have a detrimental effect on the health of your plants. A consistently strong wind can change the shape of a tree, completely altering the way it sits in a site, and this will affect the overall feel of the space.

Borrowed landscape

The canopies and roots of your neighbours' trees may have an effect on your garden, so take note of their locations. You should also consider the borrowed landscape and view from your garden – is this something you want to enhance or screen? Some of the best gardens I've seen use a borrowed landscape to their advantage. Throwing the eye out to the view beyond creates a feeling of space and drama, and – let's be honest – it has the benefit of being a maintenance-free zone!

Seasons

You need to consider the changing impacts of elements across the seasons. The sun is much higher in summer than winter, for example, and certain winds are present only at particular times of the year. Wet and dry spots may change with the seasons, too. Waiting for a whole year to pass in order to fully understand the space may not be feasible, so track the difference over a short period of time – preferably during a change of season – and expand this snapshot to cater for all seasons.

Seasonal change will have an effect on how you use the garden. An area of deep shade in summer may also get winter sun, so it'll be perfect for a small seating area. A vegetable patch may get summer sun but little winter light, so it will only be good for summer crops. Deciduous plants will lose their leaves in winter, allowing in more light when it's needed most.

Trees

I am a massive tree fan, and I love what they can bring to a garden in terms of atmosphere, screening, natural beauty, shade and habitat for birds and insects. In saying that, trees do have a few downsides: they are difficult to move, deciduous varieties drop leaves everywhere, and the roots need protecting. During your site analysis, in addition to recording the location of trees that are staying, it's important to take note of how they affect the site, too. There's a saying in the gardening world that you need 'the right plant in the right spot'. If you have a tree with the potential to grow to 20 metres (65 feet) high in a small urban garden, then I would say it's the wrong tree for that spot. When creating the garden of your dreams, consider the trees and be ruthless. If it's the right tree, keep it; if it's the wrong tree, get rid of it (subject to council approval, of course).

CREATING A DESIGN CONCEPT PLAN

WITH A FULL UNDERSTANDING OF THE SIZE OF YOUR SPACE, AND ALL OF THE ELEMENTS THAT COULD ENHANCE OR DETRACT FROM THE DESIGN OF THAT SPACE, IT'S TIME TO GET CREATIVE.

Armed with your wish list and site analysis, as well as a few copies of your base plan, head outside and imagine where you want things to go. Start by putting your ideas on paper, outlining areas of key importance, and then work through your wish list, leaving out any items that simply do not fit.

TIME TO TAKE A DIP?

Australia has more domestic swimming pools per capita than any other country in the world. If you're trying to locate a pool in your garden plan, a few factors from your site analysis will affect its placement. A pool needs to be in direct sunlight, as this allows for natural solar heating. This means steering clear of trees as much as possible, so there is less canopy shading the water. It also means that there will be little root disturbance during the construction of the pool, which is great for any existing trees.

Getting the elements down

One of the biggest mistakes people make when designing their own garden is trying to fit too much in. Getting the right scale and proportion of each element is key to making it functional. When determining how much space you need for each item, make sure you consider the area needed to move into and around the zone. For example, your entertaining area may be able to fit a 12-seater table, but if you can't pull the chairs out with ease, or stand up and move to the other side of the table without everybody else having to get up and do a little dance, then you simply don't have the space.

Movement around the key elements is the most important factor when it comes to comfortable use of the space. To help you place your items, work to the scale of the base plan and cut out bits of paper or cardboard to the shape and size of the elements you want. When placing these on the plan, include an area around the item for traffic flow. Having a tolerance between the item and the movement needed around it will give you some flexibility to overlap the items and share some of this vital space.

Despite the size of this garden, a 12-seater table would have made this outdoor dining space feel cramped.

The side of a house offers you the chance to create a dramatic pathway between the front and back gardens.

When working through your wish list, remember to add spots for planting as well as the built items. The addition of plants is what will make your space look and feel like a garden rather than just another room of the house. For small gardens, plants add texture and actually make a space feel bigger. They blur the strong lines where horizontal and vertical perimeters meet, and trick the eye into not knowing where the boundary actually is – these visual devices make the space feel larger.

Don't be scared to use the side of the house, too. Once on *Better Homes and Gardens*, we turned 24 square metres (260 square feet) of wasted side garden into a space for planting, a path and a bench seat. It doesn't sound like much, but it completely transformed the way the whole garden was used, as it became a secret hideaway where the owner could read a book in peace. The back garden could then be devoted to entertaining and outdoor cooking.

In a larger garden, plants can be used to direct traffic around the space, add unique focal points and layers of interest, and hide boundaries – making the garden look and feel even bigger than it is.

Completing the design

Once you're happy with the placement of all of your elements, including garden beds, you need to finalise your plan. Draw the outline of each element on your base plan, add the dimensions, give each element a number that correlates to an inspirational image on your mood board, and draw any defining feature of that element – for example, does your entertaining area have a roof, and what is it made of? Getting all of this down will ensure that you have considered what the element will look like, how it will work with the other elements, and how it will affect the space.

I also think it's a good idea to get nifty with a spray can at this point: take your plan outside, and mark it out on the ground. By defining the space outside, you can really get to grips with the size of the features and how they relate to each other. Making changes to your plan now is much more cost-effective than halfway through a build.

There are people who can take that two-dimensional plan and quickly and easily imagine it in three dimensions, finished and usable. Luckily for those who do not have this skill, you can now get 3D renders of your plan done for a minimal cost, by simply uploading your sketches online to a concepting company. I find that most people really benefit from seeing a plan in 3D. It's a great selling tool for the finished garden and tackles any possible issues that may not have been thought about before any construction starts. The only issue with seeing your dream garden in all its glory is that it makes you want it done straightaway – but, just like the design process, a good-quality build takes time!

5 DON'TS OF DRAFTING A LANDSCAPE PLAN

> DON'T worry if you can't draw – neither can I!

> DON'T be held back by what is already there.

> DON'T rush the process – give yourself enough time to understand the various options available to you.

> DON'T forget to allow space for movement around the garden – nobody likes to feel cramped.

> DON'T be scared to start all over again if you're not happy with the plan.

5 DOS OF DRAFTING A LANDSCAPE PLAN

> **DO** take the time to create a plan – even if it's rough.

> **DO** explore *all* of the opportunities in the garden.

> **DO** ensure that your site analysis considers all seasons of the year.

> **DO** make sure your base plan contains sewers, easements, powerlines, and water and gas outlets.

> **DO** have lots of copies of your base plan in case you make a mistake.

CHAPTER THREE

ENTERTAINING SPACES

Being outdoors is a way of life in Australia – we are blessed with incredible weather, so why not get out and enjoy it? Entertaining outside brings together all of the best things in life: good friends and conversation, delicious food and drink, fresh air and fun. Sometimes all you need to do to create an atmosphere is throw a tablecloth over an outdoor table, but having a dedicated alfresco space in which to entertain can make every occasion feel special.

You may dream of a garden with multiple entertaining spaces, large enough to accommodate different zones depending on the occasion, weather and time of day. Or you may have just enough space for one small area in which to sit and enjoy the outdoors.

No matter the size of your garden, if you plan it well you can have an incredibly functional and beautiful space that will bring you many hours of pleasure.

WHAT TO THINK ABOUT

ON THE FOLLOWING PAGES, I TAKE YOU THROUGH THE KEY THINGS TO CONSIDER WHEN PLANNING YOUR DREAM OUTDOOR ENTERTAINING SPACE.

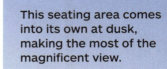This seating area comes into its own at dusk, making the most of the magnificent view.

When will you use it?

Understanding when you will use a space allows you to place it in the landscape correctly. If you intend to use it in the afternoon or early evening, you should ensure that the sun won't stream in on one side during the summer months and make some of the diners uncomfortable. Choose a location that will be as pleasant as possible for the time of day you plan to use it. If your placement choices are limited, consider incorporating shrubs, trees or a built screen to help filter the light.

This entertaining space offers both a place to eat and an area to relax. If more seating is required, it can be set up on the flat section of grass directly in front of the space.

How big do you want it?

This really comes down to how many people you are planning on feeding! If you only need to accommodate a family of four, your space can be relatively small and compact, but if you are thinking of regularly feeding 12 people, you'll need to dedicate a larger area for a table and chairs with enough space around them to have free-flowing movement. Try to allow enough room so that the space doesn't feel cramped but still maintains a feeling of intimacy, and surround it with appealing plants.

With careful planning, you can build in some flexibility as to the number of people the space can accommodate. For gatherings with just the immediate family, you might choose a small table with a more intimate feel, with the option of adding another non-permanent table to accommodate a larger party (or you could consider having an extendable table). Locating your alfresco area near some flat lawn or paving can give you the flexibility of adding this additional table without making the area feel too large when not all of it is being used.

Small can be beautiful, too.

When a friend drops by for a drink, sitting around a large outdoor dining table is fine, but you could also think about dedicating a little nook in the garden to give that café-style feel. A small table and two chairs are perfect for a guest, or even just you, and by reducing the size of the furniture you immediately make the area more intimate. Plants surround this nook in our garden, and you don't know it's there unless you squeeze your way down a narrow path – I love it, and we use it all the time.

Do you want it covered, and how weatherproof will that be?

A lot of my clients insist on having a fully waterproof outdoor dining area, and this is certainly a practical option that will allow maximum use of the outdoor space. It can be costly, though, and sometimes you lose that clear connection to the sky and the surrounding natural environment.

My outdoor dining space is covered in wisteria, which offers shade in summer and allows the winter light in – plus it also provides spectacular flowers for two weeks of the year. It is not waterproof in any way, but I love being out in the garden with the feeling of openness that it brings. I tend to think that if it's raining, stay inside! Yes, a waterproof cover can be handy if there is a shower or two and you have a planned event on, but you do lose some of the feeling of being outside.

Where should it go?

Having your alfresco area close to the inside kitchen makes practical sense. Recently though, the trend has been to locate these areas away from the house, so you are taken on a journey through the garden before arriving at the alfresco space. I love this idea but it has to be well-planned, and outdoor cooking stations and refrigeration may be necessary to make this work.

You may want to allow for a barbecue, pizza oven or meat smoker in your alfresco area. These need to be close to where you will eat, but far enough away that your guests are protected from heat and smoke. Having these areas covered makes sense so that cooking can proceed no matter the weather, but always allow for air circulation to move the smoke and grease away from the space.

When the barbecue is placed near a seating area, the chef can interact with their guests.

What sort of garden furniture?

Choosing the right outdoor furniture is just as important as plant selection in making the space feel usable and inviting. An oversized dining table or one that is the wrong shape can make a space feel congested, whereas a smaller setting will give the impression that there is room to play with. Built-in furniture is also an excellent way to make a space feel bigger, as it eliminates the need for circulation space on one side of the table.

Outdoor lounges and comfortable sofa-style seating are a superb way to indulge in the outdoors. They are perfect for when you want to enjoy a book on your own, or when you have a group of friends around and you want to relax without any formality. These casual areas can be used as breakout spaces before or after formal dining.

When selecting outdoor lounges, you really get what you pay for. Investing in quality is money well spent: the lounge has to withstand not only the rigours of everyday life, but also the harsh climate, strong UV rays and, of course, rain. Cheap outdoor furniture is a false economy, as you'll have to replace it every few years. When choosing cushions, make sure you get ones made from quick-drying foam to prevent mould growth, and that the cover fabric is water-resistant and hard-wearing. I know that you think you'll put away the cushions after every use – but trust me, you won't, and it doesn't take long before they start to deteriorate.

Stone benches are practical, as they're hard-wearing and can tie in beautifully with surrounding areas of paving or feature stones. They need to be stacked with plenty of cushions, though, to make them a comfortable option. They also work well surrounding a firepit, as the flames help to warm them up (see overleaf).

Should you have a firepit?

Dedicating an area to a firepit is a great way to extend your time outdoors throughout the cooler months. For larger gardens, you could make the firepit a stand-alone feature – it can double as a sculptural element and become a talking point. For smaller gardens, try to make the firepit a dual-purpose area, so you're not limited to using it only during cold weather. Have a removable bowl that can be replaced with a small table and chairs, and use hard-wearing paving such as crushed granite or recycled bricks that can withstand heat and timber stains. Also, avoid placing delicate plants in the area so they don't suffer in the heat.

An outdoor fireplace brings the movement of fire into a garden without taking up too much space. As it's a vertical element, the fireplace's footprint is much smaller than that of a firepit; in addition, you need to leave space all the way around a firepit, whereas a fireplace doesn't have this limitation. A fireplace is a visual magnet that will draw people together, and the chimney is a sculptural feature that will add weight to a design even during the warmer months.

Be aware that there are some restrictions about the inclusion and use of wood-burning firepits and fireplaces in residential gardens, and these differ from region to region, so check with your local council. If you live in a densely populated residential area or a fire-prone zone – or simply don't want the mess of a wood-burning firepit or fireplace – using an ethanol insert is an easy way to get the look of flames without the wood.

How much shade do you need?

In our hot climate, providing adequate shade outdoors is vital if you want to enjoy the space year-round. There are two main ways to get shade in a garden: organic and inorganic. Organic options include using trees, shrubs or climbers to create a canopy, while inorganic options include umbrellas or roof structures such as cabanas and pavilions.

There are some pros and cons with each approach. Providing a canopy with plants offers filtered light and atmosphere, but it can take time to establish and will need maintenance to keep its shape. Solid coverage with a roof ensures superior sun protection, but the hard edges can make the structure look blocky and unappealing. The ideal approach is to have a combination of organic and inorganic options to get the best of both worlds. You could use a deciduous tree and a shade sail made from soft fabric – the tree provides summer shade and lets in winter sun, while the shade sail offers the ultimate protection on the hottest of days without ruining the view with rigid edges (and it can be retractable).

A fixed shade structure, such as a pavilion, can provide a destination point in a garden that draws you towards it. When designing a pavilion, remember that it should complement the architecture of the home and the style of the garden. This structure is another roof, so it's important that it harmonises with the roofline of the house. Consider whether you're adding unnecessary bulk to the overall design, as this can congest a space and take away any views of the landscape. A skillion roof is a clever addition to many gardens, as it can be angled to minimise its impact on the design while allowing light into a space and keeping the heat out, too.

The gentle angle of the skillion roof over the outdoor entertaining space reflects that of the roof over the indoor dining and kitchen area. This visual symmetry is pleasing to the eye.

COMING AND GOING

A great garden will have well-considered 'connections': the ways in which you move from one space to the next. Put some thought into how your alfresco area will connect with the house and the rest of the outdoor space. Will you use obvious paving that is easy to follow, or subtle routes that meander? Features such as a narrowing path or soft planting at the entrance to your alfresco area can obscure the view, creating intrigue and a sense of discovery. These techniques are especially effective if you have a flat garden, as they transform a space that can be seen all at once to one that takes visitors on a journey.

What about lights?

Garden lighting is often overlooked, as the cost can seem prohibitive and many people see it as something they could do without. However, I think well-placed lighting is a real must, as it allows you to get maximum enjoyment from your outdoor space – and it looks stunning, too.

You can use lighting for functional reasons – such as illuminating outdoor cooking areas and pathways, or using sensor lights for when you're putting out the rubbish or for security – or it can be used to create mood and add drama. Large features such as trees can take on a beautiful

Lights will transform any garden into a magical realm at night. They illuminate paths, spotlight special plants and create dramatic shadows.

sculptural feel when they're lit directly from above or below; ambient light can wash across hedges and pathways; and small candle-like lights can add interest to densely planted garden beds. When it's too cold to venture out at night, looking through the window and seeing your favourite tree illuminated will give you a greater enjoyment of your garden and make the cooler months feel less claustrophobic.

Low-voltage LED lighting systems are cheap to run, easy to install and safe around children and pets. You start with a transformer to lower the voltage from the house, and then run a loop

5 DOS AND DON'TS OF GARDEN LIGHTING

> **DO** create atmosphere with shadows – these really add to the drama.

> **DO** light up your trees, but also consider downlighting with canopy lights.

> **DON'T** shine lights at eye level.

> **DON'T** just focus on practical lighting; use lighting to create ambience.

> **DON'T** overlight a space, as it will look like a shopping centre.

When spotlights are pointed up towards trees, glossy leaves shimmer at night. The trees become living sculptures in the garden.

of larger cable around the perimeter of the garden. From this larger cable, smaller wires can connect your lights to the power source. There are plenty of simple DIY kits available with easy-to-use screw connectors, or you can hire an electrician to install a system for you. I always go for a large transformer so I have the option of adding in more lights later on. For smaller gardens, you can add a transmitter to have a remote-control on/off function, and larger gardens can benefit from hooking up the lighting to a home automation system or the like for ease of use (but you'll need an electrician to install it). Solar-powered lights sound like a good idea because they're cheap and easy to install, but their light is relatively weak and almost useless for effective garden illumination.

When selecting your light fittings, try to go for the best quality you can afford, as outdoor lights have to withstand harsh elements. Unless the light is a feature pendant or wall light, I try not to think about the appearance of the light itself as much as the effect it gives. Something simple and streamlined will disappear into the garden during the day and (pardon the pun) shine at night.

What sort of shapes should you use?

You can use a variety of different shapes for entertaining spaces, and each will have a different impact on the feel and atmosphere of the design. Square and rectangular designs suit more formal gardens, and are usually easier and cheaper to install; hard materials generally come in these shapes, so you won't need to do too much cutting to make them fit. These shapes allow plenty of space for furniture, and the corners are perfect for easy installation of items such as barbecues, built-in bench seating and raised garden beds. The rectangle works better on a larger scale, as you can divide it up into smaller squares: one for dining and one for lounging, for example.

Circles allow you to surround yourself with planting, enveloping the space in a pocket of green. This shape suits both formal and informal designs, but it can be tricky when placing furniture. Semicircles give you a flat edge along which to place your furniture, yet still provide a soft, rounded outlook.

If your garden has an organic layout, with flowing gardens and lawns, it may be tricky to replicate these rounded and irregular shapes in your entertaining spaces. A curvy edge to your patio might look too over the top; however, a sweeping line may be all it needs to tie in with the design – and again, a horizontal or vertical line through the garden is all you need to use for your furniture placement. This may be a line parallel to the house or fence that gives you the balance needed.

5 WAYS TO MAXIMISE YOUR BUDGET IN AN ENTERTAINING SPACE

> Work with squares and rectangles, as there will be less cutting of hard materials needed to create a defined area.

> Select off-the-shelf products rather than custom ones.

> Minimise built structures such as pergolas and fireplaces, and replace them with things that give the same atmosphere but cost less to install, such as umbrellas and fire bowls.

> Be selective with your lighting – less is more when it comes to garden lighting.

> Don't scrimp on outdoor furniture – it's a false economy. Spend what you can but prioritise good quality.

CHAPTER FOUR

SMALL
SPACES

The small garden is the way of the future. As blocks of land shrink and houses get bigger, sadly it's the garden that suffers – so it's imperative you get the space right and make it feel as large as possible. Even if you have a big garden, there will be a corner to which you can apply small-space gardening practices, thus maximising your outdoor experience, too.

The first thing I like to do in a small space is to blur the boundary edges of the garden. When the eye is drawn to a definite boundary, such as the point where fences meet in corners and where they touch the ground, the space immediately feels smaller. Well-positioned patches of greenery will soften the visible edges of the space and remove obvious sightlines, ensuring that the space appears larger to the eye.

If this point is a junction of hard surfaces, such as two bench seats meeting in a corner, then try to break up the solid vertical and horizontal lines with some soft furnishings, such as cushions. You could also add a textural detail to the surface – decorative panelling (wainscoting) works well for a vertical surface.

96

Here, I made the olive tree the main focus. This draws you into the space and makes you forget about the size of the courtyard.

PLANNING YOUR DREAM GARDEN

BAG OF TRICKS

DECEIVING THE EYE IS KEY WHEN IT COMES TO SUCCESSFUL SMALL-SPACE GARDENING, AS THIS WILL MAKE THE AREA AS A WHOLE FEEL MUCH LARGER THAN IT IS.

A focal point such as a sculpture is a lovely way to add a personal touch to a space and draw the eye into the garden. For long and skinny spaces, try including diagonal pathways and sightlines as these will accentuate the length of the space and thus make it feel bigger.

Throwing the eye out past the boundaries of your own garden and towards your neighbours' scenery – utilising the borrowed landscape – is a great way to increase the visual size of your space. This can be as simple as incorporating the canopy of surrounding trees into your garden design.

People are often worried that plants will take over and congest a small garden area; however, the right amount of clever planting has the amazing ability to make a garden feel spacious. I like to play a trick where I use oversized foliage for my main feature plants to fool the eye into thinking the space is bigger than it is. If you do the opposite and have only small-leafed plants, then the space feels too busy and crowded. Ideally, you want a mixture of leaf textures and sizes to fill up the space yet allow comfortable movement around the garden.

CLEVER PLANT CHOICES

HAVING LOTS OF PLANTS IS GREAT, BUT YOU HAVE TO WALK THE FINE LINE BETWEEN AN APPEALING GARDEN AND AN OVERGROWN JUNGLE. YOU NEED TO BE SMART IN THE WAY YOU USE PLANTS IN A SMALL SPACE, AND TRY TO GET A LOT OF BANG FOR YOUR BUCK. SO THINK OUTSIDE THE SQUARE AND PLANT ON THE VERTICAL PLANE.

Upright plantings – such as capital pear (*Pyrus calleryana* 'Capital') and slimline camellias – work well, but using walls to your advantage is actually a smarter way to add greenery to tight places. Growing climbers such as star jasmine (*Trachelospermum jasminoides*) on wires is a cost-effective solution; better still, look for climbers that can hold themselves fairly flat against a wall and will support themselves as they grow upwards, such as creeping fig (*Ficus pumila*) or Boston ivy (*Parthenocissus tricuspidata*).

If you don't want to take up any space on the ground, you can look for a high-impact feature such as a vertical garden (otherwise known as a green wall). However, these are not for the budget conscious, as top-quality ones range in price from $1200 to $2500 per square metre! Although they're expensive, these fancy vertical gardens will really give your small garden a huge lift and draw you out into the space.

If you have a little more real estate for plants, don't be scared of including trees in your small-space garden – just be sure to select the right types. Certain maples (*Acer*

CAPITAL PEAR
Pyrus calleryana 'Capital'

STAR JASMINE
Trachelospermum jasminoides

SLIMLINE CAMELLIA

CREEPING FIG
Ficus pumila

BOSTON IVY
Parthenocissus tricuspidata

MAPLE
Acer species

species), dwarf fruit trees and specimens that can be pruned to a small size – such as crepe myrtle (*Lagerstroemia indica*) – add scale and a sense of maturity to a garden, along with a canopy that provides privacy and filtered light to understorey plants.

When looking at your remaining shrubs and perennials, research the varieties. Select the smaller and more compact ones, not the standard ones. For example, *Liriope* is a genus of strappy-leafed flowering plants that add structure to garden beds, and there are many different cultivars, from 'Evergreen Giant', which grows to 60 centimetres (24 inches) in height, to 'Pink Pearl', which reaches only 25 centimetres (10 inches) high. Choosing the right variety will give you a garden that looks well designed and not wildly overcrowded.

DWARF FRUIT TREE (MANDARIN)

DWARF FRUIT TREE (APPLE)

LIRIOPE 'EVERGREEN GIANT'

LIRIOPE 'PINK PEARL'

TOP 10 PLANTS for small spaces

1 CREPE MYRTLE
Lagerstroemia indica

2 TRACTOR SEAT PLANT
Cremanthodium reniforme

3 BLUE STAR CREEPER
Pratia pedunculata

4 NEW ZEALAND ROCK LILY
Arthropodium cirratum

5 JAPANESE BOX
Buxus microphylla

6 *CRASSULA OVATA 'BLUE BIRD'*

7 *KALANCHOE ORGYALIS 'COPPER SPOONS'*

8 *CASUARINA GLAUCA* 'COUSIN IT'

9 *CAMELLIA SASANQUA 'AVALANCHE'*

10 YEW PLUM PINE
Podocarpus macrophyllus

PLAY WITH POTS AND FURNITURE

What if you don't have a garden with soil to plant in? Perhaps you live in an apartment, with only a small balcony or courtyard in which to cultivate plants. Pots will be your best friend! Make sure you go for slimline containers so you don't take up too much space, and select plants that can cope with your aspect (which will influence the amount of sun your plants receive) as well as a limited root run.

If you want to save a few dollars, you could try a grow bag. This is a bag that contains potting mix in which plants can be directly grown, and it can hold a range of short-lived plants, such as annuals, biennials, herbs and vegetables. I actually use a grow bag to bring on my vegetable seedlings before planting them out into the veggie patch, maximising my yield.

When it comes to dressing your small space with furniture, you need to be realistic about what you can use the space for. If you don't have the room for a large dining table and an outdoor sofa to relax on, then you simply cannot have both. When selecting furniture, keep in mind that you need to be able to comfortably move around it, and don't forget the space your guests will be taking up when they sit at a table. Extension tables work wonders to transform a small garden from open patch to gathering place for friends.

Built-in furniture, such as seating, bars and tables, is also useful for the small space. This removes some of the need for circulation space, freeing up that area for other features.

Arrange a group of three complementary pots to create a pleasing vignette, or slip a single decorative pot into a snug corner.

This small space takes visitors on a meandering journey past narrow containers filled with large-leafed plants and vertical bamboo. The movement makes the area feel expansive.

5 TIPS FOR SMALL-SPACE GARDENING

> Try to hide the obvious lines in the garden – spaces where fences meet and corners form.

> Use lots of plants to make the space feel bigger, but not so many that the space is overcrowded.

> Use greenery on the vertical plane as well as the horizontal.

> Pick furniture with the right scale to suit the rest of the garden.

> Use built-in furniture and incorporate storage if possible.

PART TWO
GETTING YOUR HANDS DIRTY

CHAPTER FIVE

SOIL PREPARATION

Welcome to the dirtiest chapter of this book, as it's all about soil. For me, soil is everything when it comes to a garden. When it's good, you're in heaven and your plants will be, too. If it's bad, then it's an expensive, labour-intensive pain to fix – but unless you do, your plants simply won't flourish.

I encourage you to think about soil health in the same way you'd think about your diet: a good soil is like having a healthy diet, while a bad soil is like eating junk food all the time. Which one do you think you'd perform better on? Fertilisers are like vitamins or supplements – they can help, but they can't fix a serious underlying issue. In this chapter, we'll work out what type of soil you have and how it can be improved, as well as when and how to feed it effectively.

Soil is often overlooked, both in the home garden and on large-scale landscape projects, despite the fact that it's one of the most important things you can invest in. Sadly, the quality of our soil has been degraded over the years to the point where it no longer resembles the fertile soil of past generations. Agricultural practices (such as intensive farming and overgrazing) and environmental factors (such as air and water pollution) have led to a loss of biodiversity in our soil.

Taking steps to improve your soil may feel like pouring good money down the drain, but I promise you that the results will be obvious in the health and vigour of what grows in it. Plants are one of the most expensive elements in any garden design, so getting the soil right is your best assurance that the plants will continue to grow and look their best for as long as possible.

GETTING YOUR HANDS DIRTY

SO, WHAT IS GOOD SOIL?

THE COMPONENTS OF SOIL ARE SAND, CLAY AND SILT, AND THE RATIOS OF THESE ELEMENTS IN YOUR SOIL WILL DETERMINE HOW IT BEHAVES. FOR EXAMPLE, SANDY SOIL IS FREE-DRAINING (BUT POOR AT RETAINING WATER), WHEREAS A CLAY SOIL HOLDS ON TO MOISTURE AND NUTRIENTS (BUT CAN BE BOGGY AND SUFFOCATE PLANT ROOTS).

A good soil has an optimal mix of all three elements (when it has these it's called loam), so it drains freely yet holds enough moisture and nutrients for your plants to grow. The soil should have lots of different-sized pieces of soil (called 'peds'), leaving room for air pockets and areas to hold water. You also want plenty of decayed organic matter (sticks, dead grass and so on) and a variety of wildlife and fungi living in it.

You may have seen websites and books touting a standard ratio of 40 per cent sand, 40 per cent silt and 20 per cent clay, but this isn't ideal because it doesn't take into account the need for organic matter as well as various types of sand. Remember, too, that if you're mainly growing succulents, then you'll require a sandier mix, or if you're opting for moisture-loving plants, then you'll want more clay.

LOAM RATIO

Here's an ideal loam ratio that is versatile and suits a majority of plants:

> **10 per cent coarse sand** (big sand particles)

> **45 per cent fine sand** (small sand particles)

> **20 per cent silt**

> **15 per cent clay**

> **10 per cent organic matter** (such as well-aged manure or compost, which is always added before planting).

GETTING YOUR HANDS DIRTY

WHAT TYPE OF SOIL DO YOU HAVE?

SIMPLY LOOKING AT YOUR SOIL AND HAZARDING A GUESS WON'T TELL YOU THE WHOLE STORY. TRY THIS QUICK AND EASY EXPERIMENT TO DETERMINE YOUR SOIL TYPE.

1 Grab a handful of soil, and get rid of any rocks or twigs.

2 Add enough water to moisten the soil (it shouldn't be soaking; just wet enough so it holds together).

3 Roll the moist soil into a ball.

4 Push this ball between your thumb and index finger to form a ribbon.

1 SANDY SOIL

2 LOAM SOIL

3 CLAY SOIL

The consistency and length of the ribbon will tell you what type of soil you have.

> **Sandy soil:** if the ribbon falls apart quickly, or is less than 25 millimetres (1 inch) in length.
> **Loam soil:** the sweet spot – a ribbon length of 25–50 millimetres (1–2 inches), with a fine, smooth texture.
> **Clay soil:** if the ribbon is 50–75 millimetres (2–3 inches) then it's a light clay, and over 75 millimetres (3 inches) is a heavy clay.

You'll also need to look at the structure of the soil – the different-sized pieces, or peds, that I mentioned earlier. Peds are conglomerations of soil particles that vary in size and shape, and give soil certain characteristics. Ideally, you want a combination of small, medium and large peds.

Clay soils can contain massive peds: lumps of seemingly impenetrable clay. You can loosen a clay soil by adding gypsum, but only if the soil is unstable. To test this, simply pop some of the soil into a jar of boiled, cooled water and leave it overnight. If the water is cloudy in the morning, then the soil is unstable and will respond to the addition of gypsum. If the water is clear, then the soil is stable and will need organic matter added to improve its structure.

Discover the power of pH

The pH (power of Hydrogen) scale is used to determine the acidity or alkalinity of a substance, and it is an often-overlooked part of soil health. You can have the best soil in the world, with all of the nutrients needed for plant growth, but if your pH is off then the plants simply cannot access all that goodness.

In order to grow a wide variety of plants, you want your soil to have a neutral pH of 7. Having said that, some plants – for example, azaleas, rhododendrons, camellias and blueberries – actually prefer a soil that is slightly more acidic (6 and below). Others – such as lavenders (*Lavandula* species), oregano (*Origanum vulgare*), Jacob's ladders (*Polemonium* species) and clematis vines – like a more alkaline soil (8 and above).

Testing for pH is a simple process, with easy-to-use kits available at most garden centres or hardware stores. Correcting soil pH to obtain the optimal 7 can be done in a couple of ways. If your soil is too acidic, you can raise the level with the application of agricultural lime or aged chicken manure. If your soil is too alkaline, you can bring the number down by adding compost, iron chelates or powdered sulphur.

Your soil is alkaline if:

SOIL + VINEGAR = BUBBLES

Preferred by:

LAVENDERS · OREGANO · JACOB'S LADDERS · CLEMATIS VINES

Your soil is acidic if:

SOIL + BAKING SODA = BUBBLES

Preferred by:

AZALEAS · RHODODENDRONS · CAMELLIAS · BLUEBERRIES

GETTING YOUR HANDS DIRTY

ORGANIC MATTER

MOST SOIL STRUCTURES CAN BE IMPROVED BY ADDING ORGANIC MATTER, WHICH COMES IN A VARIETY OF FORMS: ANIMAL MANURE, GREEN-MANURE CROPS, MULCH AND, OF COURSE, THE KING OF THEM ALL – COMPOST.

Animal manure

Using animal manure from cows, chickens, alpacas and sheep is an excellent and relatively inexpensive way to improve your soil. Manure contains organic matter that helps to retain water and nutrients, and encourages earthworms and other soil wildlife to help break up heavy soils. It also has beneficial bacteria and micronutrients (such as calcium and magnesium), and increases the amount of carbon in the soil, which makes nutrients more readily available to plants – therefore boosting growth.

You don't want to apply fresh manure to your garden – it's too rich and can burn your plants. It can also contain weed seeds, which you may regret down the track. Add it to your compost pile first to help age it (and supercharge your compost!), or buy ready-cured manure from your local nursery.

Worm farms are a great way to get rid of excess kitchen scraps and create an excellent tonic for your garden. They use compost worms (not earthworms, which are very different), and you can buy these worms from the hardware store, along with the farms. These contraptions look like Daleks but are actually towers for waste collection. The worms eat your kitchen scraps, and their wee and poo collect in the bottom; you then dilute them with water (one part wee/poo to ten parts water, so the mixture is the colour of weak tea) and pour the liquid over your soil. This mixture is packed full of nutrients that can be applied all year round.

Green-manure crops

If you have poor, lifeless soil – and a little time up your sleeve – then green-manure crops are a great option. Sow a carpet of seeds from fast-growing, dense, ground-cover plants (such as mustard, lupins, soybeans or marigolds) into bare soil. Leave the plants to grow for a few weeks until they flower. Then all you need to do is slash the plants down and dig them through the soil, which allows the green waste to compost in the soil. Wait a week, and then turn the soil over again. After another two weeks, the area is ready for your permanent plants.

This process does wonders for poor soil: it suppresses weed growth, improves drainage and reduces compaction, and it rejuvenates the soil before the permanent plants go in. If you pick a legume as your green-manure crop, then it will also help to fix nitrogen for the permanent plants, giving you lush, green growth. Green-manure crops are also perfect to plant in the veggie garden after harvest, as they will bring life and vigour back to the patch before the next planting of vegetables.

1 ORGANIC MULCH *Straw*

2 ORGANIC MULCH *Bark*

3 INORGANIC MULCH *Pebbles*

Mulch

Mulch does so much for your plants and soil: it suppresses weed growth, slows water as it goes into the soil so it is easier for plants to take up, and reduces water run-off and evaporation. It also insulates the soil, keeping it at a regular temperature so that very hot or cold days are less stressful for your plants.

Mulch can be either organic (straw, bark or compost) or inorganic (pebbles or stones). On the whole, my preference is for organic – not only is it cheaper and easier to install, but it also breaks down and adds organic matter to the soil. This aids nutrient- and water-holding capacity, and improves soil structure. The exception to this is pots: I think they look better with pebble mulch, and the soil condition can easily be improved by adding in fresh potting mix.

Apply mulch to a depth of 75 millimetres (3 inches) – any less, and it's not as effective; any more, and it can prevent water getting down to soil level. This depth is also important to effectively suppress weed growth.

From a design point of view, mulch simply looks good. It can make a garden seem much more polished, as it smooths out any lumps and bumps in the soil and helps your eye to focus on the key elements and plantings.

Green waste

FRUIT AND VEGETABLE SCRAPS

EGGSHELLS

COFFEE GROUNDS AND TEA LEAVES

GRASS CLIPPINGS AND FRESH LEAVES

Brown waste

CARDBOARD

SHREDDED BLANK PAPER AND NEWSPAPER

DRIED LEAVES

TWIGS AND STICKS

Never compost

MEAT, OILS, FATS AND GREASE

FISH WASTE

DAIRY PRODUCTS

COATED PAPERS

DISEASED PLANTS

ANIMAL FAECES

TEABAGS

GREEN WASTE
*Makes up 25%
of the heap*

BROWN WASTE
*Makes up 75%
of the heap*

Compost

Compost is black gold for gardeners: it improves every type of soil and aids plant growth in a way only nature can. Plus it reduces the amount of food waste you put in landfill – it's a win–win situation!

If you're starting with a bare garden bed, digging well-aged compost and manure through the soil is the best way to incorporate them. In established beds, apply compost on top as a layer of mulch around 75–100 millimetres (3–4 inches) thick, digging it in only lightly (then the worms will do their job and drag it deep into the soil). This will roughly make up the required 10 per cent organic matter in our ideal soil mix.

Making your own compost is easy, and you don't need to have a large garden. You can use a small composting unit designed to sit on your kitchen benchtop called a **bokashi bin,** which includes a special spray to speed up the composting process and eliminate bad smells; you can opt for an outdoor system utilising a tumbler or bin; or you can create a traditional compost heap.

Regardless of the system you use, the principal is the same: you need the right combination of green waste and brown waste. The green waste includes things such as grass clippings, kitchen scraps and leaves pruned from your plants; this is considered 'wet' waste and should make up 25 per cent of the heap. The remaining 75 per cent should be brown or 'dry' waste, and this can be twigs, sticks or shredded newspapers (not pages from this book, thank you!). As we tend to generate more green waste than brown waste, I have a bale of pea-straw mulch at the ready to bulk up the brown in our compost heap.

Getting the mix right is the key to success: if it's too wet, then the heap will smell and attract fungus gnats; if it's too dry, then the heap will take years to produce useful compost. I also add a dose of compost accelerator to speed the whole thing up. But you should never add dairy products, tea bags, fats/oils, diseased plants, fish and meat, bones, pet and human poo, or glossy paper and cardboard (such as magazines) to your compost heap, as these items either don't break down fast enough, or allow pests and diseases to flourish.

Tumblers are compact and perfect for medium-sized gardens. You simply put in your brown and green waste, turn the barrel to blend the contents, and leave the mixture to compost. Each tumbler is split into two sections. Fill one side first; when it is full, leave the mixture to break down while you start adding material to the other side. After a couple of months, you can use the compost from the first side and then begin to fill it again while the second side is breaking down. You should now have a reliable source of compost, as the process is ongoing.

If you have a bit more space, then a traditional **outdoor heap** is the way to go. You'll be able to process much more waste and therefore create much more compost. The ratio of brown to green stays the same, but you need a dedicated area to create a pile. I keep mine contained with old timber pallets, as they allow the air to flow through and they keep it all somewhat neat – not that a compost heap is a pretty thing!

I have three bays: I fill the first and add to it as material becomes available; then I turn the compost into the second bay and start filling up the first bay again. When the first bay is full and the second bay is partly composted, I move the contents of the second bay into the third, and those of the first bay into the second, freeing up space for a new pile. This process not only helps to mix and aerate the compost, but also allows me to have three piles at different stages of decomposition – ideal for a continuous supply of compost.

If you don't have the space for bays like mine, then a flat spot topped by a pile of waste works just as well. You'll need to mix the pile regularly to get the compost from the inside to the outside and the non-composted material into the middle of the heap where it composts more quickly.

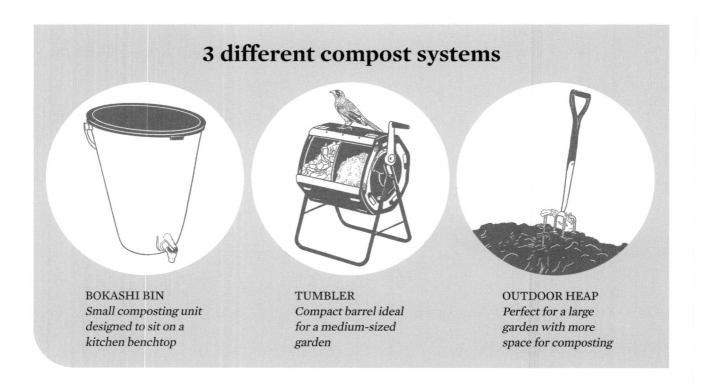

3 different compost systems

BOKASHI BIN
Small composting unit designed to sit on a kitchen benchtop

TUMBLER
Compact barrel ideal for a medium-sized garden

OUTDOOR HEAP
Perfect for a large garden with more space for composting

GETTING YOUR HANDS DIRTY

3 TIPS FOR MAKING COMPOST

> Place the bin out of sight
> Get the mix right: 25 per cent green and 75 per cent brown
> Turn your heap regularly

HOW TO MAKE YOUR OWN COMPOST BIN

Composting is an amazing way to recycle kitchen scraps and garden clippings into a nutrient-rich product that will supercharge your soil. Making a compost bin is easy and won't cost you the earth.

1 Obtain three pallets from a council clean-up or salvaged (with permission) from a building site. On a level, flat area, build three sides of a self-supporting frame to hold your compost. Join the pallets together with bugle batten screws. If you want some extra rigidity, drive star pickets into the ground at each corner.

2 You'll need a ratio of 75 per cent brown material to 25 per cent green material.

3 Mix the two together in the compost bin, adding in compost accelerator (as per the instructions on the packet), a 25-litre (22-pound) bag of cow manure and enough water to wet the mix but not to make it sodden.

4 Turn your compost every two or three weeks to bring the inside of the heap to the outside and vice versa.

5 In three months, you should have rich compost to dig through your garden beds – this should smell sweet and never sour.

Leaf mould

Leaf mould is a type of compost made from the leaves of deciduous trees and shrubs. It's not very high in nutrients, but it does improve the structure and water-holding capacity of soil. As well as being an excellent addition to homemade potting mixes, it's great for raising seeds because of its low nutrient content (just mix it with a little coarse sand); new seedling roots are tender and can burn easily in high-nutrient mixes. It is also a superb mulch for flowering plants such as roses.

As you would guess, autumn is the perfect time to make a leaf-mould pile, and it really is as easy as piling up as many leaves as possible and leaving them alone! I keep mine contained by piling them in a little pen made from old pallets with chicken wire on the sides. To collect the leaves, simply set your lawnmower on the highest setting and mow over the leaves on the ground. This picks them up and helps to shred them into smaller pieces, speeding up the composting process. I also get my children involved by making them jump up and down on the pile, so I can squeeze in as many leaves as possible.

The breakdown is a slow and civilised affair – caused by fungi rather than the heat found in a normal compost pile – and it takes up to a year. What you are trying to replicate is the natural process found on a woodland floor, so keep the pile as moist as possible (but not sodden) – a tarp over the top would aid in this.

Don't add the leaves to your regular compost pile if it's already underway; they are far too dry and will slow down the whole process to a snail's pace. Once the leaves are halfway through decomposition, you could add them to a new compost heap that has a lot of green material, as this will lead to excellent results and a quicker end product.

If you don't have a lot of leaves, or perhaps are limited with space but still want the benefits of leaf mould, try this hack. Take a large black plastic bag and stuff it with as many dry leaves as possible – really cram them in. Then half-fill the bag with water, tie the top up, and poke three or four holes in the bottom. Hide this bag behind the shed for six months, and voila – leaf mould.

HOW TO USE FERTILISERS

ALL PLANTS NEED A MIX OF MACRONUTRIENTS AND MICRONUTRIENTS FOR OPTIMAL GROWTH AND VIGOUR. A HEALTHY SOIL WITH THE ADDITION OF ORGANIC MATTER WILL SUPPORT PLANTS AND PROVIDE THEM WITH ALL OF THE NUTRIENTS THEY NEED, BUT FERTILISERS ARE USED TO SUPERCHARGE GROWTH AND GET THE BEST PERFORMANCE OUT OF YOUR PLANTS, SUCH AS LUSH LEAVES, BIGGER FLOWERS AND HEAVIER FRUITS.

Fertilisers contain a perfect combination of key macronutrients – nitrogen (N), phosphorus (P) and potassium (K) – and you'll see these expressed as the N:P:K ratio on the bag. Nitrogen is responsible for green leaves; a lawn fertiliser should have a high N ratio. Phosphorus is required for flower and fruit development, so specific fertilisers for flowering and fruiting plants will have a higher ratio of P. Potassium is in every plant cell and is important for cell health, plant strength and energy transfer, which is why it's part of the important N:P:K ratio.

Other nutrients are also important for healthy plant growth (such as magnesium and calcium), and a good all-purpose fertiliser should contain a balance of these nutrients. But often, even the best fertilisers lack some trace elements. Plants need only the tiniest amounts of certain trace elements (such as boron or molybdenum), and there is often enough in the soil to support plant growth, so these can usually be left off the ingredient list. If your soil is lacking, though, you'll see deficiencies in the plants show up as distorted leaves or unusual growth habits. In this case, an application of trace elements may be needed. I only ever apply trace elements once

a year, as I don't want to risk overloading the soil with these compounds.

The best time to fertilise is when the plant is growing. I apply a slow-release fertiliser in early spring and again in early autumn. Spring is when everything picks up again, so the need for nutrients is high; in autumn, plants are storing energy for winter so they suck a lot out of the ground. If you apply fertiliser in winter, it will simply leach through the ground and be a waste of time and money.

I also supplement my slow-release fertiliser with a fast-acting liquid fertiliser when needed. When a plant goes in the ground, I liquid-feed two weeks afterwards, just when it's starting to settle in and really put on root growth. When flower buds appear, it's great to apply a liquid fertiliser that is high in potassium, so the plant

is strong enough to build and grow larger flowers and fruits – I do this every two weeks until the buds start to open.

When it comes to fertilising the veggie patch, the key is good soil preparation, with lots of well-aged manure and compost dug through before planting. I also liquid-feed every seven to ten days during the growing season. This may seem excessive, but vegetables are heavy feeders and they thrive when given this abundance of nutrients. In addition, they are often grown in raised beds where liquid fertilisers are quickly lost.

5 WAYS TO IMPROVE YOUR SOIL

> Ensure that it has the ideal ratio of sand, silt, clay and organic matter.

> Correct the pH level so that it sits around 7 (neutral).

> Add organic matter, such as well-aged manure or compost.

> Use a fertiliser with an appropriate N:P:K ratio for the plants you want to grow.

> Double dig your soil if it's compacted.

THE ART OF DOUBLE DIGGING

COMPACTED SOILS ARE TERRIBLE FOR PLANT GROWTH. ROOTS LIKE FREE-DRAINING, LOOSE SOIL THAT THEY CAN EASILY PUSH THROUGH; COMPACTED SOILS FORCE THE ROOTS TO CURL, AND THIS STUNTS THE GROWTH OF THE PLANT. ADDING COMPOST TO THE SOIL WILL FREE IT UP AND MAKE IT EASIER FOR PLANTS TO GROW. HOW? WELCOME TO THE ART OF DOUBLE DIGGING.

Basically, double digging is removing the top layer of soil to expose the hard, compacted layer below, then digging this up to aerate it, mixing through some compost and then putting it all back. Why? Well, the more you can loosen the soil, the deeper the roots will grow. This will make your plants more resistant to drought, and you'll use less water.

First up, you need to ensure that you've slept very well – double digging is a full-on work-out, especially for your arms! Start at one end of the garden bed and move backwards. Once the topsoil is loosened, turned and aerated, you don't want to step on it again, as compaction defeats the purpose of double digging. Dig a trench across the width of the bed at the bottom end, remove the topsoil, and pile it on a tarp at the top end of the bed. This is the first dig.

Next, add some organic matter to the base of the trench – compost, manure or even leaves, twigs or mulch will do. Now comes the double dig: turn the soil over again, removing any rocks, breaking up the compacted parts and mixing through the organic matter. Once this has been done, dig out another trench next to the first, and place this topsoil in the first trench. Add organic matter to the base of the second trench, turn over the soil, and then move on to create a third trench. Keep going until you reach the top end of the bed, when the topsoil from the first trench is placed over the turned-over base of the last trench.

When you have finished, try to stay off the garden bed to keep the soil aerated. Rake it all off for a smooth, even finish. You should be very tired by now.

The good news is that this process should only ever need to be done once. If you stay off your soil to prevent compaction and simply add organic matter into the topsoil, then there will be no need to de-compact the lower layers again.

WHAT IF YOU HAVE NO SOIL?

SO, WHAT DO YOU DO IF YOU DON'T HAVE ANY SOIL, OR THE SOIL YOU DO HAVE JUST ISN'T UP TO SCRATCH? MAYBE YOU HAVE A SMALL COURTYARD, OR YOU WANT TO TURN YOUR LAWN INTO A GARDEN BED, OR YOU HAVE GUTLESS, SANDY SOIL THAT WON'T GROW ANYTHING. WELL, YOUR GARDENING DREAM IS NOT OVER! YOU COULD BUY SOIL, WHICH IS RELATIVELY CHEAP, BUT YOU WON'T KNOW WHETHER OR NOT IT'S HEALTHY SOIL. CREATING YOUR OWN GROWING MEDIUM IN THE FORM OF A NO-DIG SYSTEM IS DEFINITELY THE WAY TO GO.

You should create a raised edge for your no-dig garden – it's not essential, but the garden will get very messy if you don't. This can be made from anything, including bricks, blocks, timber sleepers, steel panels or even old pallet wood. Unlike other garden beds, the no-dig garden doesn't contain soil – you make your own growing medium instead. Making your own ensures that you get all of the beneficial microorganisms – such as bacteria, fungi, protozoa, algae, yeast and nematodes – as well as insects and earthworms, and none of the nasties (such as weed seeds).

Another huge benefit of using a no-dig system is that you don't get any compaction. Compressed ground stunts a plant's growth, as it has to work hard to get its roots down into the soil. A loose and aerated soil takes water more effectively; it works like a sponge, allowing water to soak all the way through. If soil is compacted, water simply runs off – which leaves some areas dry no matter how much they are watered.

MAKING A NO-DIG GARDEN BED

To create your growing medium,
you need the following ingredients:

> Twigs/sticks
> Agricultural lime
> Blood and bone
> Old newspapers
> Straw or lucerne mulch
> Well-aged animal manure
  or compost.

< STRAW OR
  LUCERNE MULCH

< MANURE OR
  COMPOST

< STRAW AND
  BLOOD AND BONE

< MANURE OR
  COMPOST

< STRAW OR
  LUCERNE
  MULCH

< NEWSPAPER

(GRASS)

1 Typically, you'll be putting your new
garden bed on concrete/paving, grass
or soil. If it's concrete/paving, start with a
layer of twigs and sticks to help with drainage.
If it's grass, add a good dose of agricultural
lime plus blood and bone, as this will help kill off
the grass and compost it down quickly. If you're
starting on soil, you won't need to add anything.

2 From this point, you'll be adding layers of different
ingredients to the garden bed. Each layer should
be around 10 centimetres (4 inches) deep; try not
to compact it down, or plant roots won't penetrate
the layer. First, put down a layer of newspaper
in the bed. This stops grass and weeds coming
through, so take care to run the paper up the
raised edge of the bed. It also works like a mini
reservoir, holding on to moisture.

3 Next, add a layer of straw or lucerne mulch, then
a layer of well-aged manure or compost. You can
also add green kitchen waste to this first compost
layer, but don't add it any higher up as it could
attract vermin. (If you add worm wee and poo or
rock dust to any of the compost layers, then this
will really supercharge their goodness.)

4 Follow this with a straw layer topped with blood
and bone, and then back to the compost or
manure layer. Then you simply keep layering
straw, blood and bone, manure/compost …
like you're making a garden lasagne. Aim for
a minimum of four layers.

5 The last layer should be straw or lucerne mulch,
as this is what you plant into. Create small
pockets about 10–15 centimetres (4–6 inches)
wide, and fill them with compost. You can then
sow seeds, seedlings or bulbs directly into these
pockets; vegetables and flowering annuals grow
best (in other words, plants that have a short life
cycle – so after a harvest, you can replenish the
layers to bring the level up once more). Your no-
dig garden will settle over time, so simply add
more layers to bring it back up to the right height,
always finishing with a straw or lucerne layer.

CHAPTER SIX

PLANTS AND LAWN

Gardeners have a wealth of options to choose from when selecting plants for their garden, from relatively long-lived trees and shrubs to pretty annuals, biennials and perennials that have shorter life cycles. And don't forget about lawns – a soft grassy area can contrast beautifully with busy garden beds and provide a suitable spot for ball games, pet play and picnics.

For me, plant choice can absolutely make or break a garden. A well-chosen selection of plants, suitable for the conditions, will draw you into the space and create an appealing atmosphere, making you want to spend time there. I can stare at a good garden bed all day long, taking in the different textures, heights, colours, shapes and smells. A plain, boring garden bed, on the other hand, doesn't interest me in the slightest.

Plant selection is usually driven by two factors: suitability for the conditions, and aesthetics. You might have a mental picture of what you like in terms of colour, shape and height, and then you can narrow your choices down by looking at the physical space and working out what would thrive there.

Understanding a bit about the plants you're selecting is vital to the ongoing success of a garden. Contrary to what you may believe, your plants don't want to die! As mentioned earlier, that popular saying in the gardening world that you need 'the right plant in the right spot' rings true. If you can give a plant the right set of conditions, it will perform for you.

Getting this mix of elements right comes down to researching your plants and talking to other gardeners to glean as much information as possible. You also need to be prepared to learn from mistakes. And don't take it personally – your plants don't hate you! Try to work out what factors may have influenced their decline, and learn from the experience. The more time you spend in the garden, the more you'll understand and the more you'll succeed.

CHOOSING THE RIGHT PLANTS FOR YOUR GARDEN

HERE ARE THE FACTORS TO THINK ABOUT BEFORE YOU HEAD TO THE GARDEN CENTRE.

How much sun does your plant need?

The leaves are the parts of the plant that take in sunshine and help to convert it into energy. They're sensitive to the sun, and their appearance has evolved over time to ensure that they thrive in certain light conditions. As a rule of thumb, the larger the leaf, the less direct sunlight it needs.

A plant living deep in the Indonesian jungle usually has massive leaves so that it can make the most of the very little available sunshine. If this same plant is thrust into an open garden in the suburbs, it will burn to a crisp. Likewise, an Aussie native plant with small, silvered, hairy leaves will go spindly and starve in a heavily shaded corner of the garden, because it has evolved to be more drought-tolerant and to cope with the blazing Australian sun.

WHAT'S THE DIFFERENCE?

> An ANNUAL plant grows, flowers, produces seeds and dies within one year.

> A BIENNIAL plant grows, flowers, produces seeds and dies within two years.

> A PERENNIAL plant lives for more than two years but, unlike trees and shrubs, it has little if any woody growth.

How much water does your plant need, and what soil is it growing in?

These two elements should be considered together, as the condition of the soil will dictate how much water will actually hang around, and for how long. It's how the plant copes with this amount of water that can be a deciding factor in its success. For example, rosemary (*Salvia rosmarinus*) hates its feet being wet – it much prefers good drainage and reliable rainfall. Many flowering perennial plants, such as foxgloves (*Digitalis* species) and delphiniums, like lots of moisture and nutrient-rich soil – so if you have sandy soil, no matter how much you water them, they simply won't perform. For more information on soil, see Chapter 5.

What about the environment?

External factors such as prevailing winds, the amount of reflected heat and air quality should also be considered. Think of your plants as people: they are all different – some like the beach, others the woods. I'm English, and I have a dislike for any place that is hot and windy – much like an apple tree (*Malus* species).

What and how much food does your plant need?

Vegetables and fruits are fast-growing plants, and they flower and fruit a lot, so you'll need to liquid-feed them every seven to ten days to get the best out of them. Feed a tropical perennial such as Zanzibar gem (*Zamioculcas zamiifolia*) this much, and you'll have a mushy mess of plant cells within two weeks. Understand your plants' nutrient requirements, and feed accordingly.

DESIGNING YOUR GARDEN BED

AS WELL AS GETTING THE RIGHT PLANT IN THE RIGHT SPOT, YOU WANT TO TRY TO ARRANGE YOUR PLANTS IN AN ATTRACTIVE LAYOUT. THEY SHOULD SIT TOGETHER AT THE RIGHT HEIGHTS, WITH INTERESTING COLOUR AND TEXTURAL COMBINATIONS, AND YOU ALSO WANT THEM TO CHANGE AND MOVE TO MAKE IT INTERESTING.

I have been lucky enough to chat to many of the world's best garden designers and ask them how they put together their plant palettes, and each one is different. Luciano Giubbilei, an award-winning Italian garden designer, considers the shape of each plant and the negative space created between them once they have been laid out. Michael Bates, the cream of the crop when it comes to landscaping in Australia, is all about the textures of the foliage – he feels that flowers are fleeting, so he designs based on the shape of the plant and feel of the leaves; flowers are simply a bonus.

Composition

Getting the mix of plants right and working out a planting plan is the trickiest and most creative part of garden design, and everybody does it differently.

I start with trees and large shrubs, as these living sculptures dominate any garden. They create canopy and add atmosphere, so I think they should be placed first. Obviously, you need to remember that trees take up more space and create more shade as they grow. Large shrubs form a solid block of planting compared to a group of trees; though shrubs may not get as tall as trees, this considerable mass of green will grow out as well as up.

Next are hedging plants. Hedges can be formal or informal, and are excellent for directing people around a space. They also create privacy and give you a green backdrop for the rest of your plants. Low hedges work well as borders for your planting. A judge at the RHS Chelsea Flower Show once told me that my box (*Buxus*) hedge worked as a lovely belt, separating the trousers (the paving) from the shirt (the flowering plants in the garden bed)!

After considering the placement of trees, shrubs and hedging plants, you will be left with areas of garden bed to fill with smaller plants. There are various styles that you can choose here, from mass planting to laying out plants in clumps and drifts.

Mass planting a single species creates a dramatic impact that can really take your breath away. Imagine a large swathe of Chinese silver grass (*Miscanthus sinensis*) swaying in the wind, a bank of salvia flowering for weeks on end or a carpet of low-growing roses filling the air with their perfume – you really cannot do anything but stop and enjoy the view. There are many upsides to mass planting: a single species is easier to care for, and watering and feeding regimes are more manageable when you are only looking after one species. There are drawbacks, though: essentially you have created a monoculture, so pest outbreaks can take hold quickly. And the absence of any variation in colour, texture and form can mean that the appeal is short-lived.

When planning a garden, consider using a range of plants of differing heights to add interest.

A different style of composition that adds more visual interest is planting in clumps and drifts. This creates a tapestry of plants, such as shrubs, grasses and perennials. The style is more relaxed: the plants intermingle, but individual species are planted next to each other in clumps to provide impact. These clumps can be varied in size, depending on how dominant you want a specific species to be, and are interspersed with other species to create a natural look. The placement is quite organic: you don't want straight lines, or you'll have something that looks like a McDonald's car park from 1984. You can also use stand-alone specimens with architectural qualities to punctuate and break up the flow of the drifts. For a native garden, gymea lilies (*Doryanthes excelsa*) do this really well; succulents such as agave work well in a modern garden, while topiary plants such as box (*Buxus* species) would suit a more traditional garden.

You can take this further for a softer, more show-garden look. This composition looks like it just 'happened', but is actually highly contrived, and takes a fair amount of work to achieve. It's one for the green thumbs, as you'll need to know exactly how your plants will behave together. To get this look, you need mainly perennials, with some small grasses and ferns thrown in for interest.

Start with a palette of a few favourite perennials, and plant single specimens of the same species next to each other. What you want to do is repeat these plants and mix them randomly to reflect your own personal style and preference. As you move through the garden bed, introduce something else (do it subtly by using only one of the plant), go back to the original mix, then introduce two of the new plant and then back to the original mix, and so on. Soon the new plant will be mixed through and you can start to drop some of the original combination as you have a new combination to work with. This is also the best way to move from shade to sun.

Clumps of different perennials give the garden beds a wild and untamed look that contrasts well with the formal hedges and hard landscaping.

Repeating foliage textures draws the eye through the garden.

Colour

Working with colour in a planting scheme is a great way to add interest and atmosphere to a garden bed. Obviously, there are a million different shades of green to work with, some light, some dark and everything else in between. There is also a wide range of other colours to choose from in flowers and foliage. Colour is a very personal preference, so go with what you like and what combinations you think work well.

Plants with silver foliage – such as pewter bush (*Strobilanthes gossypinus*), silver spoons (*Kalanchoe bracteata*) and *Teucrium fruticans* 'Silver Box' – tie a planting scheme together and give it cohesion.

Purple – as seen in black elderberry (*Sambucus nigra*), *Heuchera* 'Obsidian' and Chinese fringe flower (*Loropetalum chinense*) – adds drama and works as a great contrast to lighter greens, but can suck light out of a space, so always surround purple with bright foliage.

Yellow – found in lady's mantle (*Alchemilla mollis*), *Acacia cognata* 'Limelight' and *Robinia pseudoacacia* 'Frisia' – brightens any dull garden. Lady's mantle is excellent in shaded areas, as it brings in light and contrasts well with dark greens. However, when planted in open sun it can wash out, so mix it in with darker greens for maximum impact.

Silver

PEWTER BUSH
Strobilanthes gossypinus

SILVER SPOONS
Kalanchoe bracteata

TEUCRIUM FRUTICANS
'SILVER BOX'

Purple

BLACK ELDERBERRY
Sambucus nigra

HEUCHERA 'OBSIDIAN'

CHINESE FRINGE FLOWER
Loropetalum chinense

Yellow

LADY'S MANTLE
Alchemilla mollis

ACACIA COGNATA
'LIMELIGHT'

ROBINIA PSEUDOACACIA
'FRISIA'

HOW TO SAVE MONEY WITH YOUR PLANTING

WHEN DESIGNING FOR CLIENTS, I OFTEN GET ASKED TO CUT BACK THE BUDGET.

The obvious choice is to use smaller, less mature plants, as with the right care they will soon grow to become a similar size to the more expensive, full-grown options. However, this works only if you're not looking for a plant that has an immediate impact on the feel of the design. These plants are often trees and topiary plants, and they add character and atmosphere to a space. So, for these features, go big and buy for shape. It will cost you more in the short-term, but the effect on the space will be instantaneous. Don't worry, though – there are many other ways you can save money when creating a garden.

Try small but speedy plants

Buy fast-growing plants when they're smaller and less mature (and therefore cheaper), as they'll fill out quickly – and then you can spend a little bit more on mature slow-growing plants. Things such as salvias, lilly pillies, bamboos and ornamental grasses all grow pretty much in front of your eyes, so buy them small and plant them with enough space to accommodate their mature height. For slow-growing plants such as magnolias, camellias, azaleas and maples (*Acer* species), buy them a little more advanced and space them out based on 75 per cent of their mature size. This way you won't get overcrowding, but you'll still achieve a dense, textured look.

Trees and topiaries
have an immediate
impact on the feel
of the design.

5 TIPS FOR SUCCESSFUL BARE-ROOT PLANTING

> Keep the tree in a bucket of water and seawood solution until you are ready to plant it out.

> Before planting, prune up to a third of the branches to reduce the tree's stress.

> Dig lots of compost through the soil.

> When backfilling the hole, move the tree around so all of the roots make good contact with the soil.

> Create a moat to guide water to the outer edge of the roots.

Purchase bare-rooted trees and shrubs

If you're looking to save some money, you really should consider bare-rooted stock. This method of planting is one I love – the stock is much cheaper as no canopy or heavy soil is being transported around, and it's much easier to get in the ground. These deciduous trees – such as maples (*Acer* species), ashes (*Fraxinus* species) and apple trees (*Malus* species) – are dormant in winter, so that's when they get dug up out of the ground, the soil is removed from their roots, and off they go to their new home. There is a small window of time when bare-rooted stock is available in Australia. The plants need to be ordered in May or June, so they can be dug up and sent to you ready for planting out in the middle of winter.

The success of your bare-rooted stock comes down to the installation process. As you can imagine, it's a stressful process for the plant, so you need to settle the plant in as quickly as possible. Keeping it out of the ground for as short a period as possible is key. As soon as you get it home, put the plant in a bucket of water and seaweed solution to keep it hydrated until you're ready to make the move into the ground.

Before planting, you'll need to do a bit of quick pruning. The ratio of plant parts 'above the ground' to 'below the ground' has been turned upside-down during the transplanting process, as digging up the plant has involved drastically removing large parts of the root system – so try to do minimal work on the roots (snip off just the ends of the damaged ones). Remove any ripped and gnarled wood using clean, smooth cuts. Now prune up to a third of the branches to reduce the stress on the plant, as it's drawing nutrients from only a limited root system. It may seem drastic, but your plant will establish quicker and overtake a non-pruned tree in no time.

Prepare your soil with lots of compost to improve water- and nutrient-holding capacity, and dig it through. Well-turned-over soil is much easier for new roots to penetrate than compacted soil. When digging the hole for your new plant, ensure that there's an upturned cone or mound of soil left at the bottom of it. This will support the roots in a natural fashion, allowing them to splay out from the plant in all directions. The hole needs to be deep enough to support the plant but not too deep or the stem will rot; there is often a visible change in colour on the stem that you can use as a guide to determining how much of the stem should be underground. If you have a grafted plant, never cover the graft union.

Backfill your hole with your compost-rich soil, wiggling the tree to ensure good soil coverage over all of the roots. Water in well to remove any air pockets. I would also create a moat around the outer edge of the roots to hold on to water in the future; this can be filled with mulch to finish off, too.

Bare-rooted stock needs to be kept in moist, but not wet, soil. Winter rains will take care of this in most locations, but make sure the soil doesn't dry out during periods of dry weather. Feeding and additional watering should occur when the plant bursts back into life. Your new tree may also be a bit top heavy and require staking if you're in a windy area; however, I suggest removing the stakes as soon as possible to force the tree to grow stronger and stand on its own.

Create plants from cuttings

Plants are one of the biggest investments you'll make in your garden, so why not get creative and use what you or your friends already have? Propagating plants from cuttings is a cheap way to increase the number of plants in your garden, and it means that you can replace old plants with new ones that look the same without having to buy them. Cuttings also make for great gifts, and are a nice way to share your passion.

You can take cuttings from most plant types throughout the year; however, you'll have much greater success in autumn and spring when the temperatures aren't extreme.

Succulent plants such as dragon trees (*Dracaena* species), frangipanis (*Plumeria* species) and agaves respond well to being propagated from cuttings, and the process couldn't be simpler. Carefully remove a nicely shaped section from the parent plant with a sharp saw, keeping the cut as clean as possible; avoid ripping any of the bark. This mindful action benefits your cutting as well as the plant you're removing it from, as it reduces the surface area open to diseases and pests. Before putting the cutting in any potting mix or soil, you want the exposed area to scab over, otherwise it will simply rot away. Place the cutting in an area of the garden that doesn't get direct sunlight (otherwise the cutting will dry out too quickly). I like to put down some newspaper to prevent the sap from staining the ground beneath. Once there is a scab on the cut end (which usually takes seven to ten days), you can plant the cutting directly into the garden if your soil is sandy and free-draining, or into a pot with seed-raising potting mix. These types of cuttings are often top-heavy and will require some support or staking to prevent them from falling over before the roots grow.

Succulents are some of the easiest plants to propagate from cuttings.

BE A WATER WIZARD

If you live in an apartment or have a small garden, you can take water cuttings from many types of plants. Rosemary (*Salvia rosmarinus*), small succulents, geraniums, coleus and others will shoot out roots when their cuttings are simply put in a jar of clean water. The trick is to change the water every few days so it remains clear. Once your plants start producing roots, they can be transplanted out into the garden.

GETTING YOUR HANDS DIRTY

Taking a cutting from a shrub such as a salvia involves a few steps, but don't worry: it's a simple process that doesn't need years of experience.

1 Your cutting should be around 10 centimetres (4 inches) long – side shoots are best for this – and have three or four nodes (a node is the point on the stem from which a leaf grows). The bottom of the stem should be cut close to the node that will go into the potting mix, as this is where the roots will come from (it's amazing that plants can grow either leaves or roots from these nodes, depending on whether they're in or out of the soil!).

2 Using a sharp knife, remove all of the leaves on the stem except the two leaves at the top. Try not to damage the nodes when you do this, as these will grow new leaves.

3 If the two top leaves are large, snip them in half to reduce the surface area from which the plant can lose water.

4 It's a good idea to put lots of cuttings into a single pot to save space. Dip the ends in rooting powder just before you plant them (not only will this get a laugh when you tell your friends, but it also promotes quick root growth). Rather than just pushing your cuttings into the soil, slide them down the edge of the pot: this helps to increase the temperature and retain moisture around the roots, which promotes quicker striking (the term for taking root and starting to grow). The black plastic of the pot heats up, and water tends to move to the edge of the pot when you sprinkle it from above, so you get the best results when you place your cuttings around the pot edge. The potting mix needs to be free-draining; a seed-raising mix is perfect, but you can add some sharp (coarse) sand to a standard potting mix to achieve the same effect. Spraying the soil with a misting bottle twice a day will give the plant cuttings all the moisture they need to spring into life.

Use a sharp saw when taking cuttings from a thick-stemmed plant such as a frangipani (*Plumeria* species).

SEEING DOUBLE

It's easy to lift and divide clump-forming perennials such as clivias and agapanthus.

> Start by digging up what you have, trying to keep as much of the root ball intact as possible.

> Then take two garden forks, hold them so they are back to back with the bottom of the tines touching, and thrust them into the root ball. By working the curves of the forks against each other, you can pry the plant into two separate ones without damaging the roots or the base of the plant too much.

> Trim the roots with sharp secateurs so you have a 50:50 ratio of leaves to roots. If you have a small number of roots, simply reduce the foliage. Then you are ready to replant.

Grow from seed

The ultimate money saver is to grow your plants from seed. How else could you get 50 plants for $5.99? Growing from seed does have its drawbacks, though – it takes time and patience, plus you need to choose what you grow from seed very carefully. I don't grow fruit trees from seed, as you normally have to wait five to ten years to get any fruit at all. I also don't grow shrubs from seed, as you need to spend so much time in the early stages pruning them to shape that it's more cost-effective to simply buy the shape you're after.

I do, however, grow the majority of my veggies from seed. When it comes to edibles, I really like to know that what I'm eating is organic and not covered in pesticides and chemicals – growing from organic seed is the only way to ensure this.

The flowering perennials in my meadow-style garden beds are also grown from seed, as this gives a naturalistic, relaxed effect that is packed full of flowers. I simply mix a variety of seeds together, and scatter them randomly by hand rather than planting them in rows. This takes away any rigidity that the human eye might enforce. Many different seed mixes are readily available online, and they're suitable for most types of garden and climate.

Spring or autumn is the perfect time to be seeding a garden bed, away from any cold or frosty weather. First, measure your area to make sure you are applying the right quantity of seeds. Too many, and the bed will be too full and the competition from all the plants will be detrimental. Too few, and it'll look empty, plus there'll be lots of bare ground for weeds to invade. You need about 3–4 grams of seeds per square metre (around 1/10 ounce per 10 square feet).

Prepare the bed by removing all weeds and existing plants. If there are no other plants in the area, I use a non-selective natural weedkiller to do this. Spray this on as per the label, and wait for the weeds to die before removing them from the bed.

Once the weeds are gone, add compost to the soil to aid the retention of nutrients and water, plus a slow-release fertiliser such as blood and bone. Spread this over the top of the soil, and fork it through the bed. When forking the bed, break up any large earth clods and ensure that the soil is loose and friable (which basically means fluff up the soil so the new roots will be able to penetrate the ground with ease, and be able to access the well-mixed-through compost and fertiliser).

Finish by raking the bed flat and removing any large stones that have come to the surface during this process. I then mix my seeds with a carrier

Rake the bed to remove stones.

Spread the seeds by 'feeding the chooks'.

Add a thin layer of pea-straw mulch.

Use a roller to press the seeds in.

such as vermiculite or dry sand (as perennial seeds can be almost microscopic). As well as helping to distribute the seeds more evenly, the carrier holds on to heat and water where they're needed, next to the seeds. Calculating the ratio of seed to carrier depends on the seed type you're using, but bear in mind that you want the entire bed to look like it has a fine layer of dust once you've finished spreading the mix – if you're unsure, do a trial run without seeds first.

Spreading the seed mix can be done with an action aptly named 'feeding the chooks': throwing a little of the mixture out again and again, making sure it falls evenly over the soil surface. Once you are finished, spread a thin layer of pea-straw mulch over the ground's surface to protect the seeds. I then use a roller to press the seeds into the ground to ensure good contact with the soil. If you don't have a roller, lightly walking over the mulch will do this (just try not to compact the ground too much).

The final job is to water the bed and keep it moist. You don't want to flood the garden bed, but you do need to keep it consistently moist. A mist spray on a hose nozzle is perfect for this – it does take more time to effectively water the garden bed, but I think we can all agree that watering is the best job in the garden. There is something very therapeutic about it, and you can even do it with a drink in the other hand, as I often do at the end of a long day at work.

5 TIPS FOR SUCCESSFUL SEED GROWTH

> Remove all weeds from the garden bed so they don't compete with the seedlings for water or nutrients.

> Ensure that the soil is crumbly enough for small roots to penetrate.

> Mix tiny seeds with a carrier such as sand to make distribution easier.

> Lightly walk on the garden bed to ensure that all seeds make contact with the soil.

> Keep the bed moist but not soaking wet until the shoots appear.

PUNNET LOVE

When it comes to fast-growing annuals and biennials – plants that live for only a year or two, such as foxgloves (*Digitalis* species) and sweet alyssum (*Lobularia maritima*) – I buy these in a punnet. This way I get plants that have gone through the tricky germination stage but are still small, so they're inexpensive. By plucking the seedlings apart you get lots and lots of plants that will establish quickly, but you don't have the stress of germinating seeds or the expense of larger plants. It's important to keep these seedlings well watered, as the small and delicate roots will quickly dry out.

LOVELY LAWNS

THE GREAT AUSSIE LAWN IS STILL A STAPLE IN MANY GARDENS AROUND AUSTRALIA. IT GIVES US SOMEWHERE TO LIE IN THE SUN, TO KICK A FOOTBALL WITH THE KIDS AND TO HAVE A QUICK PICNIC OUTSIDE.

As a designer, I love lawn for the sense of space it can provide. It gives a feeling of openness to a garden – a breath of fresh air in contrast with densely planted garden beds. Interestingly, the average suburban lawn of approximately 90 square metres (970 square feet) can hold more carbon and produce more oxygen than the world's largest tree, so not only do families and designers love a lawn, but so does the environment.

Most established lawns do not require much water – they'll only need watering if it hasn't rained for two to three weeks, which is pretty amazing when compared to other plants. A healthy, well-prepared lawn without compacted soil shouldn't need pesticides, only fertiliser – just like other plants. If you use a battery-powered lawnmower, then this is extra good news for the environment.

With this said, I've seen some terrible lawns across the country. So how can you up your 'grass game' to get the perfect bowling-green lawn to show off to the neighbours?

3 BEST TURF VARIETIES FOR ALL AUSTRALIAN CLIMATES

> **SIR GRANGE ZOYSIA** is one sexy looking grass. It has fine, soft, dark green leaves; a slow growth rate (which equals less maintenance); and low fertilisation requirements.
> **TIFTUF HYBRID BERMUDA** has fine, dark green leaves, a high drought tolerance and a high wear tolerance.
> **SIR WALTER BUFFALO** is hard wearing and offers good shade tolerance.

Sun and soil

When you are planning a new lawn, you need to consider that grass requires a few key elements to succeed, and the top two are sun and soil. Turf grasses grown in Australia require a lot of sunshine and free-draining sandy soil, and they don't like wet feet. So when you're planning your garden layout, try to keep your lawn areas in the sunny spots. There are varieties of grass that perform well in the shade, such as Sir Walter Buffalo, but in general the rule is the more sun the better.

If you have a clay-based soil, you'll need to break it up with organic matter or gypsum, depending on the soil's stability (see page 115), and add a layer of coarse river sand for the roots to grow into. If you just add a sand layer without breaking up the soil first, you'll get a perched water table, where the sand won't drain until it's at maximum water-holding capacity. For beach-like sandy soils, the addition of organic matter will help your grass perform to a higher standard while maintaining good drainage.

While you're preparing your lawn area, it's a good idea to remove any weeds so they don't compete with the new lawn; it's easier to remove the weeds now before the grass goes down. I also remove any large stones or bits of debris to ensure a smooth base, which will give your lawn a nice, flat look.

Choosing and laying

Selecting the right variety of lawn is vital to success. Consider the amount of sun it will get, the amount of traffic it will have to deal with, the time you have to maintain it and the water it will require. I love a fine-leaf grass – it must be my English heritage – and the pick of the bunch is Sir Grange Zoysia. It's becoming more and more common on golf courses, so you know it's perfect for grass aficionados. It grows slowly, so you don't have to mow it as often, but this also means that it takes a long time to repair any damage – so if your children are rugby fans, it may not be for you. Hardy Sir Walter Buffalo is best for less sunny spots, while TifTuf Hybrid Bermuda is suitable for high-traffic areas where kids play (it's being used on football grounds around the country, so it can take a hammering). It's also a fine-leaf variety that looks very smart. TifTuf Hybrid Bermuda is the only grass with the Water Smart Australia tick of approval for drought tolerance, so it's my choice of grass for most situations.

When laying a new lawn, I always go for rolls of turf rather than seeding. It does cost a bit more, but you get a high success rate, fewer weeds and an instant effect. Start by running a roll of turf around the perimeter of the lawn area, and then stagger the rest of the rolls as you fill in the centre. This method prevents the ends of the rolls from drying out, so you won't get long, straight lines of yellowed grass.

When establishing a lawn, it is important to keep the roots moist so they will penetrate down into the soil. Watering twice daily is best for a couple of weeks, and then slowly taper off once the grass has taken root.

For existing lawns, you can teach your grass to become better adapted to drier times by watering less often but with more water – you use the same amount of water as a daily sprinkle, but divide it into one or two sessions a week. This teaches the roots to grow deep into the cooler ground where subsurface moisture sits, and to get used to long periods without rain.

SIR GRANGE ZOYSIA

SIR WALTER BUFFALO

TIFTUF HYBRID BERMUDA

HOW TO LAY YOUR OWN TURF

You don't need a professional for this job – save some money and do it yourself by following these simple step-by-step instructions.

1 Laying a lawn is all about the right preparation. Take time to get the space flat and level. Remove any stones, lumps and bumps.

2 Ensure that the soil base is free-draining; add gypsum, organic matter or sand if required.

3 Bring in coarse sand or an 80/20 mix (80 per cent sand and 20 per cent soil) to achieve your final level, which should allow for the roll of turf that will be sitting on top.

4 Compact with a water-filled garden roller, or simply walk over the entire area.

5 Use a soil spreader to achieve a smooth finish, and a spirit level if you really want the look of a bowling green. Stay off the soil once it has been levelled.

6 Apply a turf-starting fertiliser for best results.

7 Lay the turf around the outer edges of the space first to prevent the grass from drying out.

8 Fill the remaining space with turf in a staggered pattern, running the rolls across any possible slope to prevent them from slipping down the grade.

9 Use a long plank of wood to prevent excessive compaction when you walk across the new lawn.

10 Try to ensure that all edges are butted up closely. To fill in any gaps, top-dress all edges with 80/20 mix.

11 Go over the turf with a water-filled garden roller to help the plant roots make good contact with the soil.

12 Water in well, then keep up the watering as the grass becomes established – lots of water at this stage is key.

13 Stay off the grass for as long as possible, and mow it only after you see noticeable growth – start with the blades on high, and slowly bring them down to your required height.

Mowing and feeding

When it comes to 'scalping' their lawns, Australians in general are serial offenders, letting their grass get tall and then cutting it very short so they don't have to mow again for a long time. However, this stresses out the lawn, opens it up to being sunburnt and promotes weed growth. Try a different approach: raise the height of the mower blades, and mow more often. This takes off only the top of the grass, it protects the roots, and the clippings can be left on the lawn to compost down and feed the grass – what you save in time emptying the mulcher can be spent giving the grass another mow in a week!

If this sounds like too much work, do what I did and get a robot lawnmower. I named mine Nigel after a colleague and friend from *Selling Houses Australia* who is a very industrious northern Englishman. He did the daily work of ten men, just like my robot lawnmower that works every day and in all types of weather. After an initial set-up, your robot lawnmower will happily trundle about, cutting only the tops of the grass blades and improving the health of the grass and your soil.

Regular feeding of your lawn with a nitrogen-based fertiliser is a great way to keep it lush and green, and lawn-specific fertiliser has all of the other goodies it needs. It's important when fertilising your lawn – regardless of whether it's new or existing lawn – that you apply the food just before rain or water it in well using a hose to prevent leaf burn.

5 WAYS TO IMPROVE YOUR LAWN'S CHANCES OF SUCCESS

> Choose a variety that suits the location (for example, consider the amount of sun and foot traffic it will receive).

> Spend time preparing the soil well before laying any turf.

> Mow only the tops of the grass blades to avoid stressing the lawn.

> Feed regularly with a nitrogen-based fertiliser.

> Aerate the ground periodically, and remove any build-up of thatch.

Take care of your lawn, and it will reward you with verdant growth.

Show your lawn some love

As well as the ongoing maintenance of mowing, feeding and watering a lawn, it will need a periodic overhaul to keep it looking its best. This addresses the problems that can arise from compaction and overcrowding in the growth.

When a lawn gets compacted, the air is squashed out of the soil, which in turn increases the amount of water being held around the root zone of the plants. To fix this, you need to aerate the ground. You could walk on the lawn wearing special aerator sandals – silly shoes with spikes on the soles – that push through the top layer of the lawn just fine, but you really need to attack the lawn with a garden fork. Plunge the fork deep into the ground and give it a good wiggle; this will create fractures in the soil for air and water to

get into. If you have a large lawn, a self-propelled aerating machine is the way to go.

After you've aerated your lawn, top dressing is important. This stops the holes from collapsing, and maintains space for air and water. You need to use sand or an 80/20 mix (80 per cent sand and 20 per cent soil), which you can purchase from garden centres and landscape-supply businesses.

Another common issue with lawn is thatch. This brown build-up of dead leaves in the grass causes a lack of airflow, which can bring in fungal diseases, and stops water from getting to the roots effectively. You can hire a machine called a scarifier that will remove this easily. It will also rejuvenate your lawn, as it prunes the roots and promotes fresh, new growth.

CHAPTER SEVEN

MY TOP
FIVES

I often get asked about my favourite plants. The truth is that I love all plants – as long as they're in the right spot! When I was at TAFE, our teacher showed us a picture of the shrimp plant (*Justicia brandegeeana*) and proclaimed how much she hated it. She then showed us a picture of one nestled in a tropical planting scheme – and we all agreed that it looked magnificent. It was the right plant in the right spot, with complementary plants supporting it, and this made it look spectacular.

Obviously, you'll have your own opinions about what you like in a plant, and there are some species that you'll never be drawn to, no matter how well they're grown or how well they're situated in a landscape. Other plants you will love like your own children!

Here are my absolute top five favourites in each category of plants, with advice on how to make them look their best. If you're keen to add Australian native plants to your garden, then look out for this symbol next to the name. Ⓝ

TOP 5 Trees

1 CERCIS CANADENSIS 'Forest Pansy'

This is a small tree that is well suited to any garden size. It starts with purple heart-shaped leaves that turn green over the season, picking up autumnal colour before they fall. In winter, the tree shows off its zigzagging branch structure. Its real party trick comes in early spring, when the beautiful bare stems become covered in tiny, bright pink flowers. Try to keep this tree out of hot westerly winds and sun, and enrich the soil with compost before planting.

2 CREPE MYRTLE (Lagerstroemia indica)

This is a versatile small tree that, once established, copes well with heat and drought. Although it likes a well-drained soil, it will tolerate other soil types. It can be left to form a natural shape, but will also cope with a serious prune (called a pollard) on a yearly basis, so it could fit even the smallest of spaces. This tree produces a profusion of flowers in late summer and provides fantastic autumn colour, while the salmon-coloured bark looks beautiful in winter. Why wouldn't you grow one?

3 BLACK TUPELO
(Nyssa sylvatica)

This is a large, slow-growing, deciduous tree with ornamental bark and spectacular autumn colour. It can grow to around 12 metres (40 feet) tall and 6 metres (20 feet) wide, so would work best in a medium or large garden. The greenish flowers are inconspicuous, but they do attract bees to the garden; the dark blue fruits that follow are favoured by birds and possums. This tree thrives in damp, nutrient-rich soils, so plant it in a low spot or gully in the garden to maximise its water uptake.

4 MAGNOLIA

Although they come in many shapes and sizes, magnolias are all blessed with incredible flowers, some of them scented. The evergreen varieties have glossy greenish black leaves that are reddish brown on the underside, plus delicate white flowers. Large species include *Magnolia grandiflora*, which grows up to 25 metres (82 feet) tall. Smaller cultivars will grow to around 4 metres (13 feet) tall. Deciduous varieties, such as *M.* x *soulangeana*, produce purple, pink, white or yellow flowers on bare branches.

5 TRISTANIOPSIS LAURINA
'Luscious' Ⓝ

This tree grows to about 9 metres (30 feet) tall, but will achieve its full height only if moisture is reliable. If you have sandy soil, bulk it up with lots of compost and this tree will still do well. It has large glossy leaves, a white trunk similar to a silver birch (*Betula pendula*) and contrasting black stems. This combination gives you a great-looking tree that also makes a fantastic screening plant.

How to choose a healthy tree

Buying a tree will be one of the biggest investments you make when creating a garden, and picking the right variety for your conditions is crucial. Once you've done your research and decided which tree is right for your garden, look for these characteristics when you head to the nursery to ensure you are getting the healthiest and best-looking tree.

A healthy tree shouldn't look brown or dead, or have curled leaves or branches (this means it is lacking water). The trunk should taper uniformly towards the top, and the top leader – the stem pointing straight up to the sky – should be well developed. The trunk and stems should be free of scars. Branches should be uniformly distributed around the trunk, so you don't get bald spots within the canopy, and the leaves shouldn't have any holes or excessive numbers of pests on them.

Finally, ensure that the tree is not root-bound in the pot, as these roots will not spread out well when they're in the ground. The size of the tree should be in proportion to the pot size, and there should be few, if any, roots protruding from the holes in the pot.

3 TOP TIPS FOR HEALTHY TREES

- › Regularly remove any dead or damaged branches
- › Don't give mature trees too much water or fertiliser
- › Be careful when digging near trees, as you may damage the extensive root system

TOP 5 Hedging plants

1 BOX (*Buxus*)

With small leaves and a dense, compact structure, box plants knit together when pruned to give a solid block of foliage ideal for hedges. European box (*B. sempervirens*) performs well in Australia's colder zones, whereas Japanese box (*B. microphylla*) and Korean box (*B. sinica* var. *koreana*) do better in warmer areas. Box is resilient to drought once established but will need watering to get it there, and on hot days you'll notice the vibrancy of leaf colour diminish when it really needs a drink.

2 PHOTINIA

You won't have any trouble sourcing these shrubby plants, which are as tough as they come. Most species are evergreen, but some are deciduous. They tolerate most soil types, grow quickly and can be easily pruned to form medium to large hedges. New growth is bright red, and in spring the plants are covered in creamy white flowers. The fruits that follow attract many different types of birds to the garden.

3 WEEPING LILLY PILLY (*Waterhousia floribunda*)

This is my pick for a tall hedge (above 3 metres/ 10 feet), as the lime green new growth has a lovely pendulous structure that almost knits together like fish scales. Fluffy white flowers appear throughout the warmer months. Bolstering the soil during planting with lots of organic matter will help establish this tree, but it's adaptable to an array of soil types. Another good lilly pilly is *Syzygium australe* 'Resilience'; its leaves are darker, and the new growth has a blush of red.

4 YELLOWWOOD (*Podocarpus*)

The conifers in this genus are largely underutilised as hedges, partly because they're not easy to find in nurseries, and also because of their slow growth rate. They do make fabulous hedges, though, as they can tolerate both shade and sun, and will look the same in both conditions. This characteristic allows you to use them down the length of a property, from sunny spots at the front and back to shady parts alongside the house. They can also be kept narrow through pruning, so they suit the smallest of spaces.

5 ROSEMARY (*Salvia rosmarinus*)

An underutilised hedging plant, rosemary needs excellent drainage – so don't bother planting it if you are on any type of clay, unless you do a lot of work to amend the soil first. Rosemary can take all the heat that the sun has to give, and it offers the added bonus of being edible and providing flowers. It doesn't like humidity, so I would only grow it as a loose hedge. When pruning, cut into the plant on lots of different angles to create airflow – it won't ever be a formal hedge, so don't treat it like one.

A hedge will soften the boundary between your garden and the outside world.

3 TOP TIPS FOR HEROIC HEDGES

> Space the hedge plants appropriately according to the species
> Start pruning your hedge plants when they're young
> Use stringlines to get razor-sharp edges when pruning

TOP 5 Shrubs

1 VIBURNUM

This huge genus contains plants in a variety of sizes, shapes, colours and textures, so there's one to suit every style of garden. My favourites, however, are *Viburnum plicatum* and *V. opulus*. *V. plicatum* is a large deciduous shrub with a layered appearance. It is covered in creamy white flowers in spring, followed by red berries in summer. *V. opulus* is smaller, with pompoms of pale green flowers that get whiter as they get larger. Both of these species require organic-rich soil, reliable water in summer and some sun.

2 CAMELLIA

A versatile group of evergreen shrubs, camellias can be used as stand-alone specimens, in hedges or even as topiary balls. They have glossy green leaves and flowers that last from late autumn through winter. Camellias are shallow-rooted, so they suit sites that might have underlying rock. There are three main species available, each of which has a huge number of subspecies and cultivars: *Camellia sasanqua* (small leaf), *C. japonica* (medium leaf) and *C. reticulata* (large leaf). The smaller the leaf, the more sun-tolerant the plant will be.

3 *RHAPHIOLEPIS INDICA* 'Oriental Pearl'

It's almost impossible to kill this plant – it's so tolerant of wind and salt that you could literally grow it on a boat! 'Oriental Pearl' forms a lovely dense dome shape. Using this plant in a border of flowering perennials will add structure and form for the more flouncy plants to play off. It has tough, leathery, deep green leaves with little shine, which may sound dull – but this means that it's great at providing contrast and balance to a garden bed. Come spring, it will be smothered with white flowers.

4 MICHELIA

A genus of evergreen shrubs related to the magnolia, these make excellent hedges, large topiaries or stand-alone free-form shrubs in a garden bed. The glossy green leaves tolerate sun and partial shade. The real beauty of these plants is that the flowers are borne all the way up the stems, so even when hedged the shrubs still produce plenty of their mini magnolia-like blooms in yellow and cream. The flowers have an amazing scent (similar to Juicy Fruit chewing gum!).

5 BUTTERFLY BUSH (*Buddleja davidii*)

This is generally scoffed at in European gardening circles because it is a rampant weed that grows in the smallest of cracks. In Australia, though, new mini varieties for the garden have been cultivated that grow to only 1 metre (3 feet) tall. The foliage has a blue–grey tinge, and the shrub produces a mass of nectar-filled flowers that, as the common name suggests, attract butterflies and many other pollinating insects. This loose shrub suits a variety of planting styles and will reliably produce flowers in shades of purple (cultivars can be pink or white).

3 TOP TIPS FOR CHOOSING SHRUBS

> Ensure that the shrub will grow in your climate zone
> Select a shrub with a good structure, rather than the largest one in the nursery
> Check that the shrub will not grow too big for your space

TOP 5 Grasses

1 SILVER GRASS (*Miscanthus*)

By far, this is my favourite grass genus. I adore how – if the plants are positioned well – the afternoon sunlight hits the paintbrush-like seed heads, illuminating them like fireworks. There are over 150 species of silver grass and most like free-draining soil, but *M. nepalensis* can tolerate wet soils, too. Heights range from 1 to 2.5 metres (3 to 8 feet), so there will be one to suit your garden. I use the taller varieties as stand-alone features, and grow the smaller ones en masse.

2 *PANICUM VIRGATUM* 'Heavy Metal'

An upright grass, this cultivar has dull blue–grey foliage that turns yellow in cool zones during winter. The seed heads are dainty and deep pink, ageing to a bronze colour. This grass looks incredible in drifts where the blue–grey foliage complements silvery plants to tie a scheme together. It will do well in a range of soils, but prefers moist situations in either sun or light shade.

3 *CAREX BUCHANANII* 'Dusky Fountain'

This is a brown grass that can look dead if you don't place it with purpose in the garden! I like to sit this grass next to deep green shrubs such as *Rhaphiolepis* species. This makes the colour of the grass look more bronze–cinnamon and it really comes alive – the stunning contrast adds textural interest to the garden. It is extremely hardy, tolerating salt air, frost and drought well, and only requires pruning if it gets too congested over time.

4 BLUE FESCUE (*Festuca glauca*)

This small grass has blue–grey foliage and is very hardy, but doesn't like to be overwatered. Planting tufts of this grass in the front of a garden bed will tie it in with other silvery plants used in the rear and middle, and add a soft texture to the foreground. If you really want to draw the eye down to ground level, use *F. glauca* 'Elijah Blue' – it's more blue than grey, and the straw-coloured seed heads contrast beautifully with the tone of the foliage.

5 *CALAMAGROSTIS X ACUTIFLORA* 'Karl Foerster'

Growing up to 1.8 metres (6 feet) tall, this is an excellent option for adding a vertical dimension to a planting scheme. It flowers early in summer and holds its seed heads for a long period, so it can be used to punctuate a long perennial garden bed. The light yellow seed heads are full and fluffy, and they shoot upright from the grass. This makes for a dramatic effect at the back of a garden bed or a border.

Ornamental grasses add much-needed height and texture to the back of a garden bed.

How to prune ornamental grasses

Ornamental grasses are very easy to care for – you really don't need to do much to keep them healthy. In warmer regions, they will stay evergreen; in cooler regions, depending on the variety, they may turn yellow and die down in winter.

The care is the same no matter the climate – during its first winter in the ground (or when the plant looks extremely congested), simply cut all the foliage off just above ground level. This allows the plant to regenerate, and come spring it will burst back to life with fresh new growth. In subsequent years you can carry out the same pruning method, but always cut 5 centimetres (2 inches) above the previous year's pruning height to prevent damaging the plant.

3 WAYS TO USE ORNAMENTAL GRASSES

> Soften hard-landscaping areas with feathery grasses
> Choose native grasses to attract birds and other wildlife to your garden
> Plant pretty grasses in pots for unique accent points

TOP 5 Scented plants

1 GARDENIA

These come in a range of sizes to suit any garden, from large shrubs to small ground covers, but they all boast an intoxicating scent from their waxy-coated, creamy white flowers. They like sun, but I wouldn't plant them in a hot westerly position. They prefer a slightly acidic soil, so ensure that you dig lots of well-aged manure through the soil before planting. Feed them regularly, as they are hungry and need lots of nutrients to put on a good show of blooms.

2 TEA OLIVE (*Osmanthus fragrans*)

A small shrub, tea olive offers a profusion of small, white, tubular flowers that have the most magnificent scent. It is drought-tolerant once established, and requires little to no attention. It can be used for low hedging – mine sits next to my bins to eliminate odours – but be careful not to prune off the flower buds when cutting to shape.

3 ROSE
(*Rosa*)

The reigning king of fragrant flowers, roses have a scent that is the epitome of romance. In my garden I have 'Lamarque' – an old-fashioned climbing rose with a sweet scent – as well as several other lovely cultivars with scents that range from sweet apple through to dusky citrus. Roses like a sunny spot. Enrich the soil with lots of compost before planting them, and then mulch with leaf mould. Water well with drip irrigation, as overhead watering can cause fungal problems.

4 JAPANESE WISTERIA
(*Wisteria floribunda*)

The flowers of this plant have an intense scent that fills the garden on a warm spring day. It is a vigorous climber that needs room to grow, so ensure that you have a sturdy pergola or frame for it to clamber up. Japanese wisteria is deciduous so offers summer shade and winter sun, and the beautiful stalks of purplish flowers drip off the plant before the leaves emerge. The flowers are fleeting but well worth it. The plant prefers a well-drained soil and a position in full sun.

5 ROMAN CHAMOMILE
(*Chamaemelum nobile*)

This daisy-like plant is well known because you can make tea from the leaves and flowers. It makes a great ground cover in a hot, sunny spot. Grow it at the edge of a path where it can spill onto the paving, and as you step on the plant it will release its soft and relaxing scent into the garden. Like a lot of herbs, Roman chamomile likes free-draining soil, so add some horticultural grit to the planting zone for the best growth. Horticultural grit is washed grit with a particle size of 1–4 millimetres (less than 1/6 inch) and a neutral pH.

TOP 5 Ground covers

1 NATIVE VIOLET n
(*Viola hederacea*)

An excellent ground cover that tolerates most soil types, native violet is ideal for any position apart from exposed spots that receive harsh, all-day sun. It will quickly cover the ground, but does best with reliable watering. The small purple flowers are edible, and can be added to cakes or thrown in salads for a bit of interest; they don't taste like much but make a nice touch. As this plant does well in so many positions, it may take over the garden – so try to keep it contained if possible.

2 BUGLE WEED n
(*Ajuga reptans*)

Despite the terrible common name, bugle weed has small lettuce-like leaves that are actually great for adding texture to an understorey. Cultivars are available with purple as well as variegated yellow and lime foliage, and these will add interest all year round. Come spring, the plant produces bluish purple spikes of flowers that sit proud of the foliage and catch the eye.

3 PIGFACE
(Carpobrotus glaucescens)

An Australian native succulent, pigface thrives on neglect and poor sandy soils. It's excellent for binding soil together with its roots, and cooling an area down with its water-filled leaves. In addition to being a ground cover, it works well spilling over walls and planter boxes, and also has the bonus of hot pink daisy-like flowers to add a pop of colour. Propagation couldn't be easier – simply place a cutting on the ground, sprinkle it lightly with soil, and away it goes.

4 JAPANESE SPURGE
(Pachysandra terminalis)

This evergreen plant has deep green foliage and thrives in shaded areas such as under trees. It doesn't mind competing for nutrients with other plants, and provides a lush greenness in dark places where most plants simply can't grow. Tiny white flowers appear on spikes above the foliage during spring. Prepare the ground before planting by loosening the soil and incorporating organic matter where possible, as this will give it a boost while it establishes.

5 TRAILING PRATIA
(Lobelia pedunculata)

A miniature ground cover, trailing pratia has tiny leaves and starry white or mauve–blue flowers in spring and summer. This plant does well in most soil types, though it likes water so struggles a bit in sandy soils. I like to use it between stepping stones – both formal and informal – and to fill in gaps and crevices, as it supplies reliable greenery and flowers. It can also be used as a substitute for lawn if it doesn't get too much traffic.

TOP 5 Flowers

1 PEONY
(Paeonia)

These are my favourite flowers; they are blousy, fragrant, romantic and simply stunning. I love them so much I even have them tattooed on my arm! Peonies come in a wide range of colours and textures, from single flowers to ruffled doubles. They can be difficult to grow in Australia, and are only really suitable for the cooler regions (I have tried in Sydney and failed). If you do have the climate for them (I'm jealous!), enrich the soil with lots of compost and a large handful of lime before planting.

2 BLUE MIST FLOWER
(Bartlettina sordida)

An amazing large-leafed shrub, this grows well in shade or light sun, and reaches up to 2.5 metres (8 feet) high. Come spring, this soft, hairy shrub is covered in pompoms of purple flower heads that bring interest and light to an understorey. This plant is easy to care for: when it's thirsty, it will tell you by wilting; it quickly bounces back after a drink. I recommend mulching under the shrub, as it doesn't like to dry out every day. Prune it after flowering, and feed during the growing season with an all-purpose fertiliser.

3 HYDRANGEA

These have made a comeback recently – they are now appreciated as garden stunners, and no longer thought of as 'granny' plants. They grow best in morning sun and afternoon shade so they don't burn. If you don't have a spot like this, then grow them in a pot so you can move them into a shady spot in the afternoon. Many species are chosen for their ball-like flower heads, but look at *Hydrangea paniculata* for its cone-shaped flower heads, *H. quercifolia* for its foliage, and *H. petiolaris* for its climbing ability.

4 MASTERWORT
(*Astrantia major*)

If you prefer easy-to-grow flowers, then this is the one for you. This perennial likes both shade and sun, and will cope with a variety of soil types, too. It doesn't require much help once established, growing to about 60 centimetres (24 inches) tall. The pretty flower head resembles a pincushion: a mass of tiny flowers on stems poking out from the centre and surrounded by petal-like bracts; you can find cultivars in white, green, pink and purple. This plant appears in almost every self-respecting herbaceous border.

5 LILAC
(*Syringa*)

These are stunning large shrubs that grow between 1.8 and 4 metres (6 and 13 feet) tall in the right location. They have fragrant flower clusters in pink, purple or white that are quite showy. Position them at the back of a garden bed where they can get to full height, or use them to line a garden path where the fragrance can waft around you as you walk past. Lilac likes a cool climate, but can also be grown in a pot so you can move it to cooler parts of the garden during the year. It's a bit of work, but well worth it.

TOP 5

Textural delights

1 *KALANCHOE ORGYALIS* 'Copper Spoons'

This is a succulent shrub-like plant that looks, as the cultivar name suggests, like copper spoons. Growing around 1 metre (3 feet) in height, it has a branching upright appearance that goes well with a variety of plants or impresses as a stand-alone feature in a pot. The leathery foliage and interesting colour make for an excellent combination in any garden, and the plant will contrast with almost everything around it. Bright yellow flowers appear at the branch tips from late winter to spring.

2 *CASUARINA GLAUCA* (n) 'Cousin It'

A low-growing ground cover, this plant is a cultivar of the tall swamp oak (*C. glauca*). Dense foliage spreads across the ground, forming a low mound. It creates a sea of textural greens when planted en masse, but also works well as a single plant spilling over a pathway or into an entertaining space. Although the swamp oak is native to the east coast of Australia, don't be fooled into thinking that the cultivar is drought-tolerant – this plant requires a lot of water to establish and stay looking deep green and healthy.

200

3 CRASSULA OVATA 'Blue Bird'

Also known as the blue jade plant, this has grey–blue foliage that forms bun-shaped mounds. It is one of many jade cultivars on the market, each with their own textural difference and interest. This one can tolerate lots of sun, poor soil and sand, but doesn't like too much water around its roots. Combining jade plants in large clumps will give you the look of a coral reef, or you can plant 'Blue Bird' on its own in a pot of a contrasting colour for an eye-catching feature on a deck or in a courtyard.

4 SPURGE (Euphorbia)

Euphorbia is a huge and diverse genus of plants ranging from tall cactus-looking plants through to flowering subshrubs. They are all easy to grow, although the sap can be a skin irritant, so watch out when handling them. I like *E. characias* subsp. *wulfenii* because of its twirling blue–grey foliage and the brilliant yellow flower heads that appear in spring and summer. It looks great in the front or middle of a garden bed, and provides fantastic textural interest all year round.

5 TRACTOR SEAT PLANT (Cremanthodium reniforme)

This is a shade- and moisture-loving plant, although it can tolerate some sun. It has the most fantastic leaves that stand upright and proud, and look just like old-fashioned tractor seats. The electric yellow flowers appear in late autumn and early winter, high above the interesting foliage. Both the shape and the arrangement of the leaves make this plant a textural darling; however, the gloss on the foliage will draw the eye as well.

3 TOP TIPS FOR CHOOSING TEXTURAL PLANTS

> Create interest by using a mix of different textures
> Consider how light and shade will affect the appearance of a texture
> Site spiky plants away from pathways and garden edges

TOP 5 Yellow plants

1 ROBINIA PSEUDOACACIA 'Frisia'

A tree with an open appearance and rounded lime leaves that turn golden in autumn, this cultivar can grow up to 10 metres (33 feet) tall. It will tolerate some shade so is excellent for bringing light to a woodland area. For the smaller garden, it can be pruned to form a 'mop top' to provide a formal look – this is ideal if you need something for a sightline or point of interest. This tree produces white pea-like flowers that develop into long black seed pods.

2 ACACIA COGNATA 'Limelight' n

This native dwarf cultivar has delightful weeping foliage that cascades into a dense bun shape, forming bright lime green–yellow mounds. It likes free-draining soil and a sunny spot but can tolerate some shade. It requires very little maintenance as far as watering and pruning go, and only needs a native-specific fertiliser in spring to retain the vibrancy of the foliage colour. I like to use these en masse to create a sea of golden textural foliage.

3 LADY'S MANTLE (*Alchemilla mollis*)

This is a low-growing plant, similar to coral bells (*Heuchera*); however, the foliage can be slightly fuller, giving it a more abundant look. This plant tolerates shade and sun, but it will burn if it's in a spot that is exposed to harsh all-day sunlight. It will thrive in the majority of soils (though it doesn't like soils that are waterlogged). Lime green foliage and masses of delicate yellow flowers combine in this bright and attractive understorey plant that borders pathways beautifully.

4 ACER PALMATUM 'Sango-kaku'

A medium-sized maple tree, this cultivar will work in the ground or in a pot – so it's perfect for gardens of any size. Similar to most maples, it doesn't like hot westerly sun, and will require organic-rich soil and plenty of moisture in summer, but it's worth growing. The yellow-tinged foliage combines with coral-coloured bark to offer a visual and architectural plant for the garden. In autumn, the leaves turn bright golden yellow with a hint of orange.

5 SHELL GINGER (*Alpinia zerumbet*)

This is a large-leafed plant that can grow up to 2.5 metres (8 feet) in height. The variegated forms come in a range of colours, from stripy green right the way through to shocking yellow. Because of the height and colour, it's best grown at the back of a garden bed where it can bring interest to a shaded, easy-to-lose space.

TOP 5 Purple plants

1 SMOKE BUSH
(*Cotinus coggygria*)

A large shrub with rounded leaves, smoke bush grows in most positions and soils but prefers well-drained, sunny spots. Some popular cultivars – such as 'Royal Purple' – have stunning purple foliage that adds visual interest to garden beds. Its common name relates to the pale, wispy flower plumes; when contrasted with the foliage, they look like smoke. Like the crepe myrtle (*Lagerstroemia indica*), this shrub can be pollarded (given a serious prune) to maintain a certain size and shape.

2 CORAL BELLS
(*Heuchera*)

This is a genus of small perennials in an array of colours, from yellow to green through to purple and almost black. My preference is for the darker tones, and they sit nicely among plants in lighter greens and silvers. The plants produce small, bell-like flowers that sit above the foliage, but it's the texture and colour of the leaves that is really appealing. Plant in a sunny spot, water well, and feed with a nitrogen-rich fertiliser for extra leaf growth.

3 *SEDUM* 'Purple Blob'

The purple is found on the outside of the leaf rosettes, contrasting with a silver tone on the inside. Being a succulent, it can handle sun and dry feet, so it's perfect for a pot where it can spill and blob over the edge. It also works well planted next to a path, where it can encroach and add textural interest. A fast-growing ground cover around 15 centimetres (6 inches) in height, it is low maintenance once established. Starry yellow flowers appear in summer.

4 BLACK ELDERBERRY (*Sambucus nigra*)

A few cultivars of this large shrub have deep purple leaves that look dramatic in the garden. However, having a large amount of dark foliage in a garden bed can suck a lot of light out of it, so this shrub needs an open spot where it can really be shown off in all its glory. The dark foliage makes a great background for the abundant pinkish white flowers that eventually become elderberries later in the year – be quick if you want to eat them, as the birds get to them early!

5 CHINESE FRINGE FLOWER (*Loropetalum chinense*)

This versatile shrub can be trained into various shapes, which makes it ideal for hedging or adding a rounded mound to a garden-planting scheme. As well as a lime green variety, there is a purplish plum form that makes a delightful contrast to surrounding green and yellow plants. Both types have the added bonus of soft, fringe-like flowers in either white (for the green variety) or electric pink (for the purple variety). This shrub can be grown in sun or full shade; however, the growth of specimens in shade will be slow, and you'll need to prune to promote a dense habit.

3 WAYS TO USE PURPLE PLANTS

> Place purple plants next to light green or yellow varieties for contrast
> Add drama to any planting scheme with a purple swathe
> Combine different shades of purple for visual interest

TOP 5 Silver plants

1 *COTYLEDON ORBICULATA* 'Silver Waves'

This low-growing silver succulent looks like shimmering coral when it is mass-planted in a garden. It is fantastic for adding textural interest to the lower sections of a garden, or as a stand-alone feature in a pot or in a row of troughs on a balcony. It needs excellent drainage and full sun to thrive, but will cope with summer heat and winter cold when established. This cultivar grows well from cuttings, so this is an easy way to increase the number of plants in your garden.

2 PEWTER BUSH (*Strobilanthes gossypinus*)

This shrub has a brown, slightly hairy tinge to its silvery foliage, and a beautiful leaf arrangement that makes it attractive to look at. I find it's very effective when used in various locations around the garden to tie a planting scheme together. The foliage is dense at the growth tip of each stem and then spreads out as it ages, giving an upright look to the leaves. You can create new plants by taking cuttings, if you reduce the leaf size by half to minimise water loss (see pages 158–61 for more information on cuttings).

3 COASTAL ROSEMARY
(*Westringia fruticosa*)

A native shrub with very small, dense, blue–silver leaves, this can be left to grow into a natural shape or pruned into more formal topiary forms. It needs lots of sun to prevent it from becoming leggy (having long and straggly stems), and it will not tolerate wet soils, so plant it at the top of a slope or in a hot westerly position. Be careful not to over-fertilise it, as it doesn't require the same amount of nutrition as plants such as roses. When treated right, it will reward you with plenty of small, lilac–blue flowers.

4 RUSSIAN OLIVE
(*Elaeagnus angustifolia*)

With silvery foliage that feels slightly rough to the touch (like fine sandpaper), this large shrub or small tree is perfect for hedging and topiary. It also has to be one of the fastest growing plants out there. It's incredibly drought-tolerant, so it's great for low-water gardens, but it can also tolerate wet soils. I like to use this as a bit of a statement by planting a series of large balls in a lawn or open area – their unique tone and interesting texture create a great atmosphere.

5 *TEUCRIUM FRUTICANS*
'Silver Box'

This compact and hardy shrub is perfect for hot, windy, free-draining sites. The bright silver foliage contrasts well with greens, and can really draw your eye into a planting design and hold your attention. The shrub has an interesting growth habit of crisscrossing branches, so it's better used as medium-sized hedging or pruned into organic shapes and balls – unless, of course, you want to add the textural element to your garden design.

5 QUESTIONS TO ASK YOURSELF BEFORE ADDING A PLANT TO YOUR GARDEN

› Can I give this plant the maintenance it needs?

› Is it the right size (at maturity) for the space?

› Will it get enough light?

› Will it thrive in my particular climate zone?

› Does it suit my garden style and the plants that will surround it?

Conclusion

For years I have known the benefits of getting out in the garden, both physically and mentally. I weed the garden as my meditation practice. I used to get frustrated when I couldn't finish weeding because I was sidetracked by young children or demanding clients. However, as soon as I realised that weeding is a job that is never done, I started to zone out and enjoy the process. Weeds will always grow, and their removal is just one of the many jobs that will always need to be done in the garden.

While I was writing this book, the world went through a global pandemic. During that time, I saw a change in people's desires and priorities. The importance of having a garden had never been appreciated so much. The escapism, the connection with nature and the role that gardening plays in improving mental health have been saviours for all those who like to get their hands in dirt.

Gardening has increased in popularity, and for good reason: it makes you feel good, it is deeply satisfying and it gives purpose to your day. Like weeding, the task of learning about gardening will never be completed. There will always be new plants to discover, new practices to put in place and different circumstances to overcome.

For those who are new to gardening: welcome to a lifelong hobby that will enrich your existence in so many ways. Please do not get put off by killing a few plants; the compost that feeds my garden is made up of many plants I have killed! Each time you will learn more about your garden – just try not to make the same mistake twice. Study your plants as they grow, and watch how they react to the different amounts of sun, water and food they receive. In time, you will understand that the way they grow tells you what they need.

For seasoned green thumbs: you know what you have, and I hope you enjoy imparting your knowledge to the new generation of gardeners that has emerged through these tough times.

Acknowledgements

To my beautiful wife, Juliet. Thank you for supporting me, no matter what I do. Thank you for understanding when I disappear into the garden for hours on end, and thank you for helping me to pull this book together despite all of the other 500 things we are doing at the moment. Without you, I couldn't be me. I love you more than anything, and I love that we will grow old together in a garden somewhere.

Moggie, who would have thought that I would have a career in gardening or even write a book on the subject? I remember all those years ago when I refused to move rocks for you in your garden, and how I found your overgrown courgettes disgusting. Now I love having you in my garden, even if you are rubbish at pruning and you turn all of my sculpted topiaries into odd-looking cubes! Thank you for being the best mother and for supporting me ... even if I'll never be Alan Titchmarsh.

Creating a lot of the gardens you see here in this book is a team effort, and I am very lucky to have a great team around me. Thank you to the staff at Inspired Exteriors. Each project starts with the design team that helps to transform my concepts into highly detailed plans, which the construction team implements to the highest standard. Watching these gardens grow with the maintenance team is a true pleasure in my life; not many jobs allow you to take a thought and watch that develop into a living, breathing organism that clients enjoy.

To the team at Murdoch Books, including but obviously not limited to Kristy Allen, Virginia Birch, Sarah McCoy, Breanna Blundell, Dannielle Viera, Julia Cornelius and Trisha Garner, thank you for holding my hand through the process and turning my often dribble into this beautiful book that I hope you are as proud of as I am.

Thank you Cath Muscat for your stunning photographs, especially those you shot at my farm. I will forever treasure them as they capture so perfectly the moment in time.

Finally, to Jane Morrow. You approached me a long time ago to write this book and I put it off for so many years! I couldn't be happier now it's here in front of my eyes – thank you for persisting with me and thank you for all your help and expertise along the way.

Index

GARDEN OF YOUR DREAMS

Published in 2022 by Murdoch Books,
an imprint of Allen & Unwin

Murdoch Books Australia
83 Alexander Street
Crows Nest NSW 2065
Phone: +61 (0)2 8425 0100
murdochbooks.com.au
info@murdochbooks.com.au

Murdoch Books UK
Ormond House
26–27 Boswell Street
London WC1N 3JZ
Phone: +44 (0) 20 8785 5995
murdochbooks.co.uk
info@murdochbooks.co.uk

For corporate orders and custom publishing,
contact our business development team at
salesenquiries@murdochbooks.com.au

Publisher: Jane Morrow
Editorial Manager: Virginia Birch
Design Manager: Kristy Allen
Design: Sarah McCoy, Kristy Allen and Trisha Garner
Cover Designer: Sarah McCoy
Editor: Dannielle Viera
Photographer: Cath Muscat
Illustrator: Julia Cornelius
Stylist: Juliet Love, Inspired Interiors
Production Director: Lou Playfair

Photographs: 103(ccr), 200(c) by Adobe Stock Images
© Adobe Stock; 36–7, 100(bl), 100(br), 103(t), 103(cll),
103(br), 153(tl), 183(c), 187(b), 191, 192, 194(c), 195(t),
196, 197(b), 198, 199(c), 201(c), 201(b), 204, 205(t),
205(b), 206, 207(t), 210(b), 211(t) by Alamy Images
© Alamy; 38 by Nathan Burkett © Nathan Burkett
Landscape Architecture; 101, 159 by Mark Burrough
© Burrough Photography; 100(tl), 100(cr), 153(bc), 170,
178, 179(t), 179(c), 182, 183(b), 186(b), 187(t), 187(c),
190(b), 195(c), 199(b), 205(c), 207(c), 210(c), 211(b) by
Dreamstime Images © Dreamstime; 157 by Flemings
Nurseries © Flemings Nurseries; 21, 84–7 by Murray
Fredericks © Murray Fredericks Photography; 156 by
Getty Images © Getty; 16–17, 23, 48–9, 55, 56–7, 59,
61, 67, 74–5, 80, 90–1, 138–9, 155, 184–5 by Natalie
Hunfalvay © Natalie Hunfalvay; 100(tr), 117, 153(tc),
153(tr), 153(cr), 183(t), 190(c), 194(b), 197(c), 199(t),
207(c) by iStock Images © iStock; 150–1 by Matt
Keightley © Matt Keightley; 68–9, 173 by Jason Martino
© Jason Martino; 72–3 by Jason Martino and Robert
Lipman © Jason Martino and Robert Lipman; 82, 102,
142–3, 148–9 by Adam McDonald © Adam McDonald;
42–3 by Ali Mentesh © Red Cow Farm Garden; 97 by
Michael Nicholson © Michael Nicholson Photography;
64–5 by Graham Rowe © Graham Rowe; 4–5, 14–5,
100(cl), 103(crr) 108–9, 153(cl), 153(bl), 153(br), 186(c),
195(b), 197(t), 200(b), 214–15 by Shutterstock Images
© Shutterstock; 39, 166–7, 192, 193 by Amelia Stanwix
© Amelia Stanwix; 24–7, 40–1, 88–9 by Joshua Marshall
Whitby © Joshua Marshall Whitby; 32–3, 51, 209 by
Mark Vessey © Mark Vessey.

Murdoch Books wishes to acknowledge the following
individuals and companies, whose work appears in
this book: 21, 84–7 by Bell Landscapes and Clinton
Cole, CplusC Architectural Workshop; 150–1 by Matt
Keightley, Rosebank Landscaping; 82, 102, 142–3,
148–9 by Adam McDonald, Impressions Landscape;
101, 159 by Edward Warburton, Greenwall Solutions;
39, 166–7, 192, 193 by Philip Withers.

ISBN 978 1 92235 178 4

 A catalogue record for this
book is available from the
National Library of Australia

A catalogue record for this book is available from the
British Library

Colour reproduction by Splitting Image Colour Studio
Pty Ltd, Clayton, Victoria

Printed by C&C Offset Printing Co. Ltd., China

10 9 8 7 6 5 4 3 2 1

MIX
Paper from
responsible sources
FSC® C008047